Y0-AGK-261

Earth, Fire and Air

Walter Kraul

Earth, Fire and Air

Playful Explorations in the Four Elements

Floris Books

Translated by Donald Maclean

First published in German as two volumes under the titles
Spielen mit Wasser und Luft and *Spielen mit Feuer und Erde*
by Verlag Freies Geistesleben in 1984 and 1985
First published in English in 1989 by Floris Books
Third edition published in 2010

© 1984, 1985, 2006 Verlag Freies Geistesleben & Urachhaus GmbH, Stuttgart
This translation © Floris Books 1989, 2005
All rights reserved. No part of this publication may be reproduced
without the prior permission of
Floris Books, 15 Harrison Gardens, Edinburgh
www.florisbooks.co.uk

Coloured drawings by Reinhart Heinsdorff
Photographs by Peter Schreyer and Walter Kraul
Except fig 2, Christine von Königslöw; fig 58, Irmgard Kutsch;
fig 68, Deutsches Museum, Munich; fig 72, Helmut Brunner;
fig 81, Rolf Durschner; fig 98, Theodor Schwenk;
fig 136, Kunstmuseum Bern.

British Library CIP Data available
ISBN 978-086315-768-4
Printed in China

Contents

Introduction

Children are drawn instinctively to play with water, air, fire and earth, and given the chance will play imaginatively for hours with these elements. The purpose of this book is to show how this can be encouraged and developed. It is written more for parents and teachers than for the children themselves. The best activities are those where the child comes into direct contact with earth, water and air, but sometimes it is a toy — preferably home-made — which brings the child into this kind of contact. The construction of some of these toys is described, though not in too great detail.

Some of the simplest toys are suitable for a three-year-old child, while others are complicated contraptions which will only work properly after patient trial and error. No special indications are given as to which toy is suitable for which age: this has to be found individually.

The first encounters with the elements will be simple, but as children grow their scope and skill will increase. Older children will play with younger ones, the older ones perhaps making something for the younger ones to play with. Parents can play with the children or simply watch them. It may be that adults will play themselves, for the elements allow serious people to become children again. While this book is not directed at a particular age group, some play activities can be dangerous where the elements are strong, so adult supervision is necessary.

1

2   *A small brook — an ideal playground.*

1. Playing with Earth

Whereas the elements of water and air can be played with directly, earth and fire can usually only be played with indirectly; but no less enjoyment can be derived from them on that account. Playing with the elements always involves a certain risk and this risk has to be eliminated, therefore the kind of play must be adapted to the age of the child, and their skill and experience taken into account.

Every activity that has to do with matter, and particularly with weight, we shall regard as playing with 'earth', whether used to drive a machine, if it is overcome intelligently or felt particularly strongly.

Direct play with earth takes place in the sandpit or on a sandy beach. With this element you can build all sorts of things, and sand mixed with water can be given a certain degree of firmness. Later, this play can be transformed into a more serious activity if the child is allowed to look after a flowerbed in the garden. Older children can be taken to visit caves or mines, which are profound experiences of earth.

Any mass that can be modelled, whether it be clay, Plasticine or beeswax, offers the chance of getting to grips with earth. With these substances artistic forms can be created, admittedly on a smaller scale, but with greater possibilities than in the sandpit. Also different colours are available. In winter where there is snow children love playing with it and know how to use it: they make snowmen, snow castles and caves, and throw snowballs at each other. All this is playing with earth insofar as earth represents all that is solid.

Then there is wood. Wood can be pictured as earth raised by the plant to bear leaves or needles. Even a less practised hand can carve toys out of wood as used to be done in peasant houses in the long winter evenings, when people were less demanding and children had powerful imaginations. In old books you can still find examples of remarkable toys. In toy museums one can find delightful examples like a herd of cattle made from bits of branches. In Waldorf (Rudolf Steiner) kindergartens the children play with bits of wood as they appear in nature, or even better with bits of roots. All this is playing with earth in a wide sense.

4

5   *Playing with marbles*

The earth as a whole is a sphere. It is reflected in miniature by the ball. So really every ball game is playing with the earth, whether it be catching and throwing or whether one is bouncing the ball. It is all playing with gravity. The same applies to playing with solid balls, marbles, bowls, skittles, billiards, croquet or, in winter, curling. There are classic toys which should not become forgotten. For example, there is the tumbler in all sorts of variations, and the top in all shapes and sizes, the yo-yo climbing up a string after being jerked, and the hoop kept upright as it is bowled along. Apart from the tumbler all these toys require skill and practice. They all overcome gravity and so are cause for astonishment, or are we so numbed today that we can no longer wonder at simple phenomena?

Before I begin to describe individual toys I must mention the swing in all its variations, as seesaw, as rope-swing or at a fair as swingboat that goes round. On a swing you experience weightlessness for a moment at the highest point and a correspondingly greater weight at the lowest point. There is a similar experience in whizzing downhill in a soapbox on wheels.

6   *Go-kart*

Stone towers

Hikers will have come across the stone towers marking a path in the mountains. Sometimes there are more towers than necessary — obviously someone has been having fun here.

Children love building stone towers, and it can become an art form. They will sit in silent concentration building these structures, almost as if the stones themselves tell them how.

7   *Building stone towers by a river*

8   *Towers built by children*

9 *Stone towers in the Alps*

Collecting stones

Everyone loves collecting things, and some collect stones, the hardest form of the element of earth. Pebble beaches or riversides are often uncomfortable for walking barefoot, but for the stone collector they are a paradise. The movement of the waer has rounded the sharp edges of the stones and made them into smooth pebbles.

Stones with white veins are pretty. Sometimes they have a cross (figure 10). You can arrange them into patterns like circles or spirals (figures 11 & 12). You can leave them in the sand for others to admire. Sometimes you can find stones with a face, or with a little help they will show their face (figure 13).

In some places you can find precious or semi-precious stones. With some luck you might find a crystal. You might know a rock collector who can show you where to find good stones.

11   A stone spiral

12   A stone circle

10   'Cross stones'

13   A gnome's face

13

Guessing weights

This game is suitable for a child's birthday. Take the kitchen scales, then collect all kinds of objects of different sizes and shapes, all about the same weight but made of different materials: pieces of metal, wood, cardboard, stones, cloth. They can be toys, books, cushions, crockery, articles of clothing and even foods. Now you need to ask only two questions: which object is the lightest, and which the heaviest? The answers can be quite wrong! The biggest article can be the lightest and the smallest the heaviest. The children can weigh them in their hands before the scales determine who is correct.

Domino downfall

Children everywhere enjoy making things fall over. Dominoes are particularly effective (figure 14). By setting the dominoes up in a row then letting one fall against the next thus knocking it over and so on, a whole series with bends and angles in it can be made to fall down. In 1984, a student in Germany took 280 working hours to set up 300,000 dominoes. At night, the work had to be protected from mice. It took eighteen minutes for most of them to fall over as planned, a new world record. Even without a record, making things fall over is fun, like knocking down a tower of blocks that took a lot of trouble to build: although the tower falls in a heap while the dominoes fall in the way that was intended.

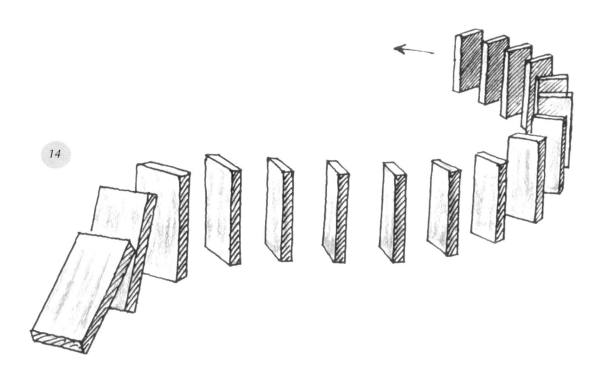

14

The tumbler

This toy is the opposite of the dominoes in that it does not fall over. A good handyman can easily make a tumbler, especially if he has a small turning lathe.

The tumbler is round below, ideally a complete hemisphere. The upper part of the tumbler is made as light as possible. You can put a basket on top and let your child put weights in the basket (figure 15). The tumbler begins to rock more and more slowly until at last it falls over. If you take some of the weights out of the basket it will stand up again.

You can make a simple tumbler with a table-tennis ball. Cut the ball in half, fill one half with sand, close it with a cardboard lid and put a lightweight doll on top.

The yo-yo

It is not difficult to make a yo-yo, and an amateur woodturner will find it fun. If you do not have a lathe you must find two equal discs, or cut them out with a fret-saw. The discs must not be too thin, since they must act as flywheels to a certain extent to enable the yo-yo to climb up the string. Cardboard discs are not heavy enough. The insides must be perfectly smooth otherwise the string will rub against them and act as a brake. The discs are joined together by a wooden peg in the middle to which a piece of string, or preferably spun nylon line, has already been attached. The line should be about 3 feet (1 m) long with a loop at the other end, and then the yo-yo is made.

15

16

Tops

Tops should be made by turning on a lathe. They will spin well and for a long time if a round-headed brass upholstery nail is driven into the bottom. Earlier generations started their tops off and kept them spinning with a whip, or played with a diabolo, also known as 'devil on two sticks', which is a double cone made to spin in the air by means of a string attached to two sticks, one held in each hand. If you do not have a lathe you can take a wooden wheel from an old toy pram and glue a beechwood peg into the axle hole, paint it brightly, and there is your finished top. If you give this type of top a fairly long shaft it will have a remarkable characteristic: spin it inside a box, and the walls do not stop the spin when the top hits them, but instead knock the top away. There are games developed from this. Inside a box — an old drawer is very suitable for this — build some partitions with gateways in them and place the box on a slight slant. Wind the string on to the top, place it in a special holder at one end of the box, and set it spinning. The winner is the person whose top gets through most doorways (figure 17).

Another kind of top can be made from a wooden sphere. It has the surprising ability to turn over while it is spinning and stand on its point (figure 18). This little miracle only happens if the upper part of the top is not too heavy, so it should be hollowed out with a thick drill and a little spindle set in it for setting it off. If the top is painted, this will give interesting effects before the top stands up.

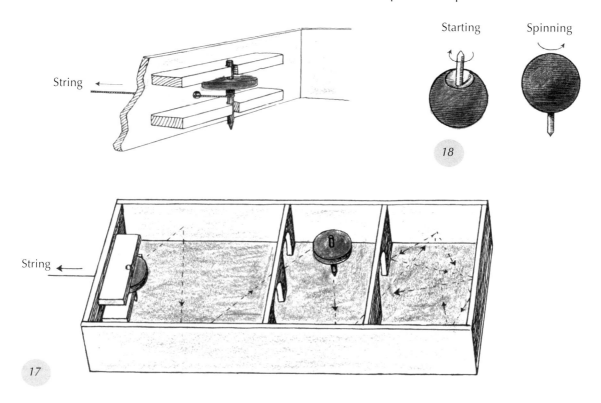

String

Starting   Spinning

18

String

17

16

A Japanese top game

Tops are remarkable things. There is an especially interesting version from Japan: a flat top which spins in the middle of a 'wooden plate' with a raised rim. Along with the top there are two little wooden discs (figure 19). These are

19

big enough to lie on the top while it is spinning and are taken round by it. Seen side-on the discs are shaped differently and are also slightly different in size. This causes one to overtake the other by slipping under it. We mention it here only as a curiosity.

The Zaptarapp

This is simply made. Take an orange wrapped in paper, or wrap it in tissue paper. Shape the paper to make a 'hat' that completely covers the orange right down to the table. If you like, paint a face on the paper and there is your Zaptarapp, alive and ready. Give him a push on a smooth table and he will run about in remarkable movements because of the irregularity of the orange.

20

The cotton reel

When your mother is knitting and her ball of wool falls to the floor, you might try to pull it towards you by pulling the yarn so that you can then pick the ball up without having to get up. Usually the ball only unwinds some more and runs further away, but it is quite different with a reel of thread, especially if it is nearly empty. If you pull it cleverly by the thread it will come rolling towards you and even wind itself up, but the thread must wind on from below and you must pull very low. Unfortunately, large wooden cotton reels are becoming rare. You can make one yourself out of a round piece of wood and two discs of the same size. The greater the difference between the diameter of the round piece of wood and that of the discs, the better it will work. The reel should also have some weight. One might make a game by getting some suitable reels of the same size and seeing who can best wind on the thread.

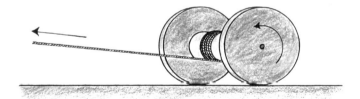

21

The walking men

With this toy a weight serves to make two walkers move. Figure 22a shows a model of this kind. The weight hangs by a string over the edge of the table. The two little men are joined rigidly together and wobble from side to side, thus changing their weight from foot to foot. The legs are slightly movable, and so the little men take a step forward every time they wobble until they reach the edge of the table, where they promptly stop. They never fall over the edge.

It is tremendously difficult to make the men, and it may need several attempts, but it can be done. The weight and size of the men, their centre of gravity, the mobility of their legs etc. must all be balanced up exactly. The feet are rounded along the side of the soles. What a triumph for the craftsman when the men finally do walk like clockwork right to the edge of the table.

Another traditional plaything is the walker on the sloping plank (figure 22b). He walks down, having one movable and one fixed leg. He has to be balanced out so that he wobbles slowly downhill like the two men with the weight and string. This time the man's own weight makes him move. This plaything also requires many patient trials until it works perfectly.

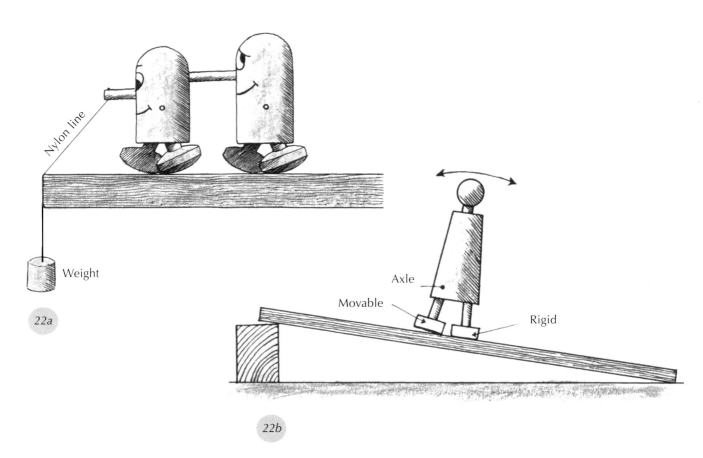

Nylon line

Weight

22a

Axle

Movable

Rigid

22b

18

The acrobat on parallel bars

An ancient toy is the acrobat swinging along two slightly sloping parallel bars. This toy can be bought, but it can also be made without much trouble. The bars are mounted on a board so that they slope gently. Cut the acrobat out of a piece of plywood. Insert a round rod through him, slightly off his point of balance. You can also paint the acrobat on a disc or simply use a disc, but the axle must be set eccentrically (off-centre), otherwise the disc will just roll smoothly down the bars, not rhythmically which is much more fun. To start him off the acrobat will sometimes need a little push.

You could make the bars quite long so that the ends touch the ground and see what happens when the wheel lands on the ground still rolling.

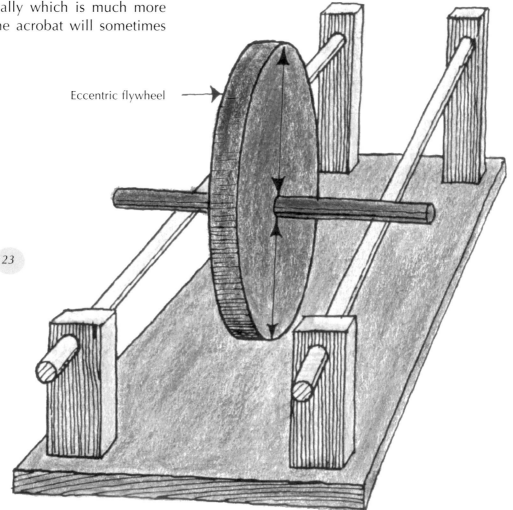

Eccentric flywheel

23

It can be fun to make a marble or a ball roll down a prescribed route to the bottom of a run. This we shall call a "marble run". You can buy them ready-made, but then you lose the best part of the fun which is trying the thing out to see if it works. Can you get a ball to gather enough momentum to clear a level part, or even go uphill again? Will it jump out of the run if it is going too fast round a sharp bend? It is exciting to adjust a home-made marble run until it works properly.

There are many ways to make one. Firstly, you can buy ready-made conduits with bevelled joints for the bends. The conduits are simply laid end to end in a sandpit. But if you want to make the whole thing yourself you do not have to have a router, you can nail side slats to each side of the flat bottom slat, wide enough apart to take the balls which you are going to use. To make the

bends just saw off the ends obliquely. This kind of gutter gives the balls a very sure run and it is almost impossible for them to jump out. You can make the runs even more economically by nailing or gluing square slats on to the top edges of a flat slat. For the bends it is enough if the far side has a side (figure 24b). With this system the bends are always rather unsatisfactory as they have steps, but for the sandpit they are quite sufficient. Two conduits, one laid on top of the other, make an excellent tunnel which can be dug into the sand.

The balls can be porcelain or glass marbles or you can get steel ball bearings of any size. Those of inferior quality are cheaper. Steel balls are heavy and so roll particularly well. But even at home you can find adequate balls, for example, round wooden beads or even peas. As we have said, the width of the run must be suited to the

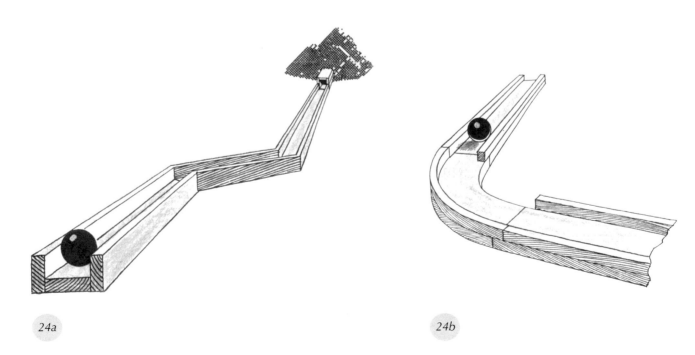

24a

24b

balls, but it is surprising how wide the run must be for a particular ball.

So far I have dealt with wooden gutters laid end to end, but you can vary the run, although it must be said that the problem lies in the bends. Hoses or tubes are the first variant, and a run can consist entirely of tubes, but then the ball is completely shut in and there is no risk of it jumping out. A combination is possible: straight pieces as open wooden gutters, with the bends in flexible tubes, for instance, electricians' tubing or an old garden hose. It is up to the skill of the builder to join up tubes and gutters. For this rubber bands can be used (figure 25).

Such a run does not have to be in sand, it can be built on a sloping field and the gutters supported by sticks stuck in the ground. You can do without the bends of tubing if you allow the ball to drop from one gutter to the next (figure 26).

In winter we can still go on building marble runs. A pile of snow is an ideal basis for gutters of all types, but you can also build a marble run indoors. Every good playroom has building blocks of all kinds, or you can use boxes or books as supports for the gutters. The problem is to make the gutters firm, especially if you are rolling heavy steel balls. Adhesive pads or tape, elastic bands or even paper clips are useful. For indoors you can make good bends with cardboard and stick them on to the wooden gutters.

It is often difficult to keep an unwell child in bed but you may succeed by giving them the equipment to build a marble run. Give them a good platform such as a board, a piece of plywood or even strong cardboard, some stiff paper (such as drawing paper) and a pair of scissors, some glue and some little balls, for instance, a bicycle ball bearing.

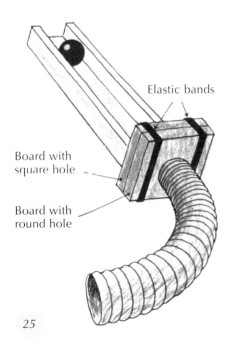

Elastic bands

Board with square hole

Board with round hole

25

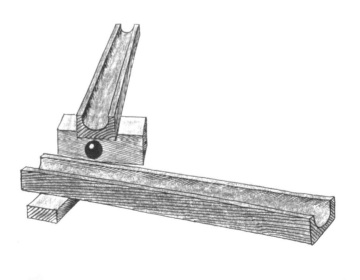

26

Always build marble runs from the bottom upwards, but first make an open box out of paper for the balls, so that they do not get lost in the bed. The first paper gutter ends in the box. Make the gutters from strips of paper. These can be folded in one of three ways:

1) V-shaped gutters: place a ruler along the centre-line of the strip and fold one half of the strip over the ruler.

2) U-shaped gutters: fold one third of the strip over the ruler, then fold the opposite third over the ruler.

3) Semicircular gutters: wind the strip lengthwise round a pencil or rod.

The supports are also made of paper. To prevent them from buckling fold them lengthwise to make an oblong box. In building construction, the same technique is used with sheet metal.

The child will want to make bends. It is quite easy to bend the V-shape. Cut a piece for the bend out of paper and crease it with your hand bit by bit and bend it, and then your bend is ready (figure 27).

The U-form has to be cut in from the side. Bend the flaps up and stick them together with long strips (figure 28). The semi-circular kind cannot be bent easily.

Stick the first bend on to the straight piece and give it a fresh support. Proceed backwards until you have made the whole run. The whole thing looks like a switchback (figure 29).

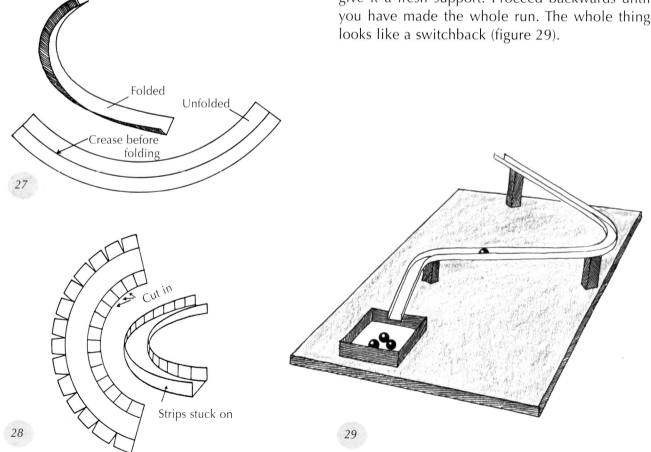

Folded

Unfolded

Crease before folding

27

Cut in

Strips stuck on

28

29

22

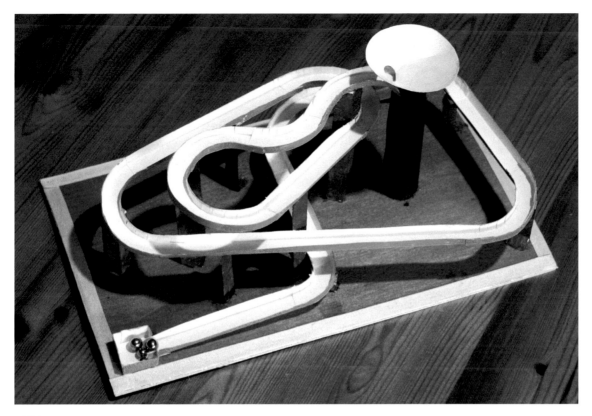

30 Marble run made of paper

A paper marble run made by the child 31

Every new piece added to the run must be tried out before proceeding further. Several alterations may be needed. A piece may have been set too steeply so the ball jumps out at the next bend; or it may be that the ball gets stuck somewhere and needs a steeper incline to give it more momentum. To prevent the ball jumping out at the bends, the sides of the bends can be heightened by adding extra strips. If the supports collapse they must be strengthened or made more stable by joining them together. Fit a small paper funnel at the top where the ball goes in to give it a better start. If the run will not stand firmly, use a wooden rod here or there to steady it.

Once the run is finished, the child can start rolling the balls, one after the other, and see if one can catch the other. Usually it is possible to build a second run in the first framework. That makes a splendid complex. There are all sorts of possibilities; fast runs and slow runs. You might like to use bamboo cane which is suitable material for a marble run made of natural materials.

One good variation for all runs is a little dip. The ball then gathers momentum and goes over the next hump. If you put a ball in the dip and let another equally heavy ball roll in from the top, it will cause the first one to move on, while the second one remains stuck. You can try this out with several balls.

You can carve a run out of wood (figure 32), but you need a lot of patience. Alternatively the element of earth in the form of clay can serve as a run (figure 33).

You can also make a run using stiff wire, but that needs skill in soldering or welding.

32   A wooden marble run

33   A clay marble run

34 Rolling eggs

Rolling eggs

Variations of this game are found in many countries. In one version coloured Easter eggs, as hard-boiled as possible, are rolled down a run. The run consists of two similar shafts laid close together. The egg rolls down on to a field where there are already other eggs, at which point each child lays a penny on their own egg. The new egg has to be started with such skill that it hits as many other eggs as possible, knocks the pennies off the other eggs and in the course of this does not get cracked. The height at which the egg is launched and the way it is laid on the run (where the pointed end and where the round part lie) determine the way in which the egg rolls in the grass.

The displaced pennies belong to the last child to set off an egg; the pennies are collected and one of them placed on the last child's egg which has now joined those on the grass. The next child takes their egg from the grass and sets it off to try the same again. If your egg breaks during the game, you can get another, but you are allowed only one egg at a time in the game.

The slide

Until now all these rolling balls did not push anything, we just had fun with them, but you can use the tendency of a ball to run downhill to push something. The vehicle can be a matchbox. You can make the run out of strong paper or light cardboard. Make a broad U-shaped channel somewhat wider than the matchbox. Try out a straight run first in order to ascertain the required gradient. Let a steel ball (diameter about ³/4 in, 20 mm) roll behind the matchbox. Place a little doll inside the matchbox. Now make the bends. To stop the box from getting stuck the run must

be wider on a bend. You do not need an inside wall on the bend as the ball will stay on the outside because of its centrifugal force. A little box, narrower at the front and covered over, looks better, and can be made easily. It is best with an indentation at the back to take the ball. For this kind of run the supports should be built of slats. An even incline is recommended. To make it more attractive you can paint it and you can make a cash kiosk, because the dolls are not allowed to slide down without paying. It might even be possible for you to make a conveyor belt to take the vehicle from the kiosk to the top. Then you just put the ball behind it and the journey down begins.

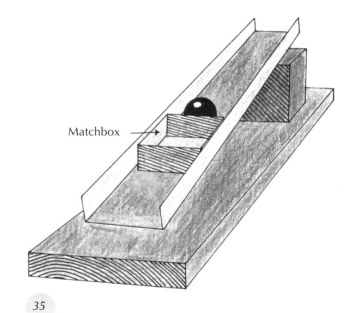

Matchbox

35

26

The gravity car

The slide can be developed further. Stick a loop of paper in front of the matchbox and put the ball inside. This time use a tray as a base. As you tip the tray slightly the ball runs down and pulls the matchbox after it. A further development might be to fix two little wheels at the back and close the front. The hood covers the heavy ball which is the engine and this makes the whole affair mysterious. The ball will rub against the cover and the sides, so it is a good idea to lubricate these parts on the inside with graphite (lead pencil). Now the gravity car is finished. Of course, a doll inside reminds us of the dodgems at a fair.

Now the whole thing can be made much more exciting by taking a flat board (plywood is the best) and building obstacles on it: blocks, traffic cones, road signs, archways, tunnels and even a garage. The board must have a surround to it otherwise the car will easily fall off. And now we can drive through the countryside, without polluting the environment, by moving the board so that gravity works.

The somersaulter

The somersaulter is an ancient toy that keeps on coming back into vogue. He will turn somersaults on any inclined plane. What makes it work is a heavy ball in the hollow head. If you make one yourself you will only succeed if you keep the following points in mind.

Take as heavy a ball as possible. For his head take a cardboard cylinder somewhat wider in diameter than the ball and about twice as long. Place the ball inside the cylinder and close the ends by attaching some strong material. The rest is a matter of artistic design. Cut out a body with outstretched arms and legs, the top part of the body should be double thickness. Stick paper over the cylinder and paint a jolly face on it. Now stick the head into the upper part of the body. Sew or stick the body together, adding hands, feet and even a cap or beard and that is the somersaulting dwarf ready (figure 37).

36

37

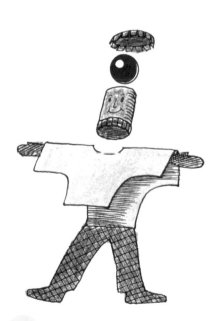

The incline on which the toy is to turn somersaults must not be slippery otherwise the somersaulter will just slide and not turn properly. Any board with a cloth over it will do. It is interesting to guess how much slope is required to make the thing work. The little man will also turn somersaults on a pillow, on the ironing board, on a deckchair, on a slope in the garden, and children will find other places. You can sometimes buy somersaulters.

You can also have fun experimenting with balls in little boxes of different sizes. The boxes will move in remarkable rhythms down inclined slopes.

38

The earth-moon game

With wooden balls 1 to 2 inches (3 to 6 cm) in diameter, you can make a good and instructive toy. Attach eye screws to two balls and tie them together with an elastic band (figure 39).

Now hold one ball in your hand and let the other swing round in a circle on a table. In this way the elastic twists up and the toy is wound up. Now place both balls on a table-top and give them a little push. The balls will revolve round each other.

It becomes more interesting if we take balls of different sizes. The little ball makes a big orbit and the big ball a little orbit. The balls revolve round their common centre of mass (figure 40).

What do we learn from this? We have a model showing the motion of the earth and the moon. The earth (large ball) holds the little moon as if on an invisible rubber band and pulls the moon round itself, much more slowly of course as it takes about twenty-eight days.

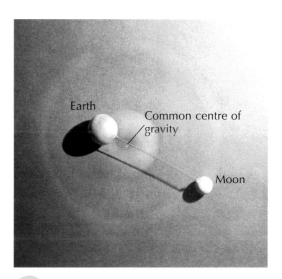

40

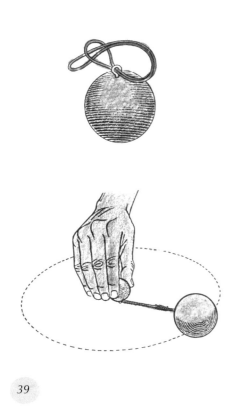

39

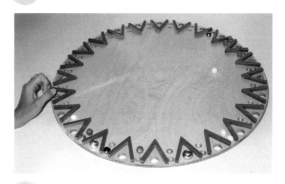

41   Tióbolo game, available from www.tiobolo.de

29

Funiculars

A funicular is a cable-railway that is on a steep track. The car is hauled by a cable. Usually there is a second car on the other end of the cable, so that when one car is ascending the other is descending. The cable goes round a wheel at the top. You can construct a toy on this principle.

Start with a smooth board. Set it up on an incline, for instance, leaning against a table. Then you will need a car that can be loaded. Tie a string on to the car which you have chosen and you can pull the car up the board. You can have a doll sitting in the car. Now make a winch with a pawl and ratchet-wheel so the action can be stopped and the car held at any stage of its ascent (figure 42).

Now you can winch the car up. For the car to descend into the valley again you have to disengage the pawl and use a finger as a brake. The car rolls down by itself due to the force of gravity. Expert engineers will fit a mechanical brake on to the winch. Of course you can build a special car with seats set at the correct angle for the incline, as is the case with real funiculars.

Once you have achieved this you can think of the other funicular which you make with two cars. It does not matter what kind they are. In this situation you won't need a winch, but you will need a large pulley wheel round which you pass the cable, or you can take two smaller wheels set far enough apart to prevent the two cars bumping

pawl

42

into each other as they pass. The wheel should have a handle so that you can turn it, and the cars need guide-rails, say two slats outside each set of wheels. But if the car has rimmed wheels on one side one slat for each car can be the guide-rail (figure 43).

Now the traffic up and down can begin. As one car travels up, the other travels down. If the top car is heavier than the bottom one, both cars will be self-propelled! As a weight you can use a suitable stone. Once the car has come to the bottom the stone must be taken out and put in the top car so that the journey can start all over again. Be sure to put the brakes on in time (figure 44)! In real life funiculars are built with one track except in the middle where the cars pass each other. But it is better not to try to copy this; you will not succeed with this kind of model, as the friction is too great.

You could drive your funicular electrically if you have a small motor and the necessary skill.

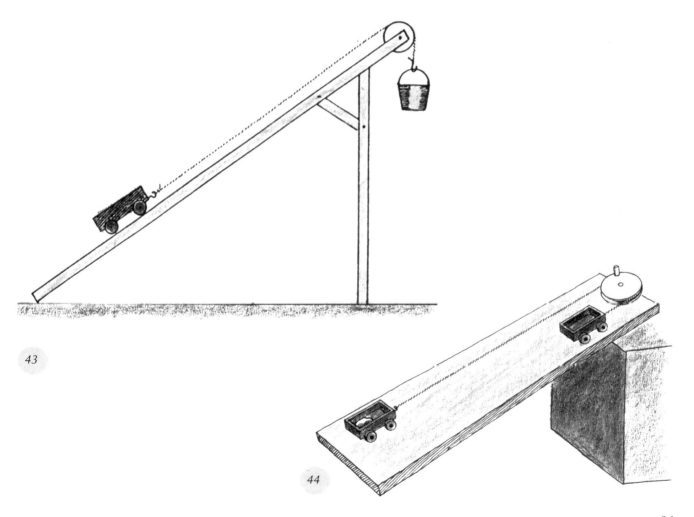

43

44

Self-propelled cable car

Unlike the funicular these cars run on cables. The cars must be equipped with easily running pulley wheels. Take care that they hang straight. You can, of course, make the cars in any shape or size that you choose — even a gondola with a roof can be made. When the car is finished, tie a string tightly on to a suspension point. Hold the other end and put the car on it. If you raise the end which you are holding the car will run away from you. If you lower it the car will come back. Its weight makes it go.

Now take a long cord (cable) and stretch it between two points and let the car travel by itself. At the bottom either the cable is slack and goes up again and the car comes to a stop or, if the car does not travel too fast, it can be stopped by the branches of a tree. To get the car back up, pull it by a piece of string tied to the traveller. You can build supports for the cable, and if you do this cleverly the car will run over the supports without jumping off the cable.

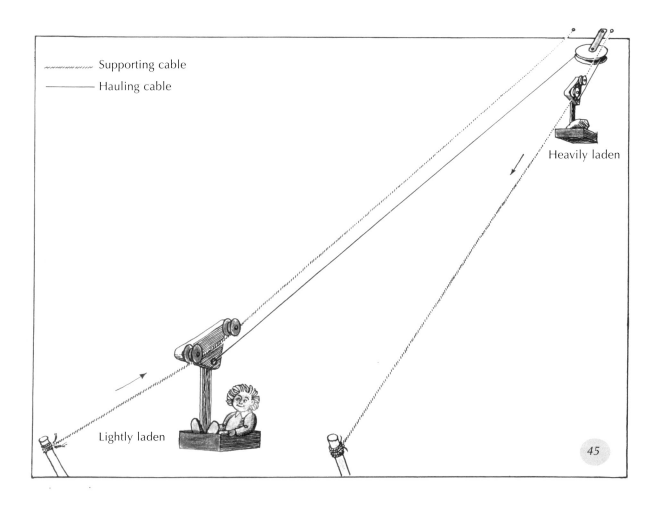

~~~~~~~~~~ Supporting cable

———— Hauling cable

Heavily laden

Lightly laden

45

In a self-driven two-car cable system there is one difficulty. Once they are set off they will accelerate and they will have to brake before they reach their destinations. Hang the cables slack so that they are steeper at the top and become more level at the bottom. This makes for good operation. The top car, as already described in the funicular, is loaded heavily and so draws the lighter bottom car up, for they are both attached to the same hauling cable. This cable also passes round a wheel at the top of the mountain. When setting off the top (driving) car has a good start because of the steepness and it can accelerate both cars. When it comes down to the flatter part of the cable it loses momentum and both cars slow down.

By careful and patient experiments you can make the cars stop exactly at the stations without braking and without any outside interference. Children might like to make houses at the top and bottom stations, or the child sitting at the top can collect a heap of stones and the one at the bottom can put dolls and surprises in the car to be transported automatically up to the top.

The doll elevator

Place two grooved wheels above an overhang (figure 46). Lay a string across them and attach a basket to either end of the string. Put a doll in one basket and a weight in the other. As the weight pulls its basket down, the doll will be lifted up.

46

The ball wheel

A ball wheel is an automatic marble run. By means of a weight the balls are brought up to the top of the device in compartments of the wheel. The mechanism runs by itself. Before the ball falls into the bottom rill it rolls over a key which it presses down by its weight. This key is mounted on a seesaw, on which there is also a peg (figure 47). This peg catches on a projecting spoke and checks the wheel. As the seesaw dips, the peg releases the wheel. At the same time a second peg on the other side of the seesaw rises and checks the wheel again. Because of a counterbalance the seesaw now returns to its original position and the wheel is again checked by the first peg, but it has moved round by one chamber, and so for the ball which has arrived there is an empty chamber ready.

At the same time all the balls in the wheel are raised by one spoke, and a fresh ball drops from the top chamber. If the weight has a drop of three feet the contraption will run for about an hour. Of course beforehand many hours of intense experimentation are necessary to make this ball wheel run fairly well.

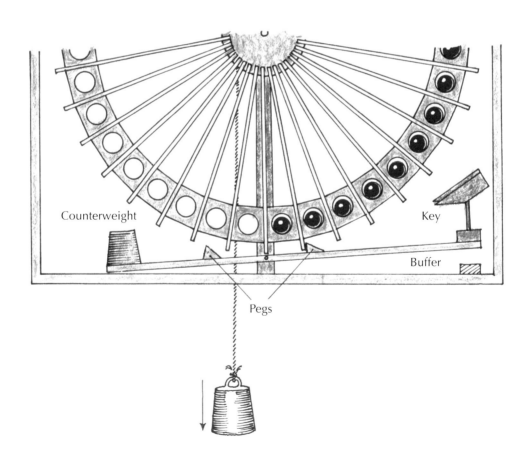

Counterweight   Key

Buffer

Pegs

47

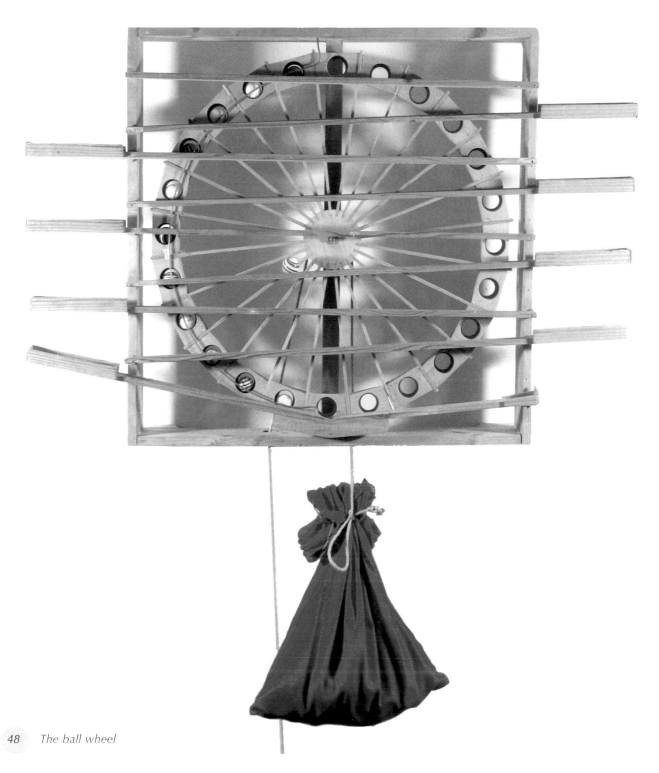

48   *The ball wheel*

The ball seesaw

Like the clock this device is driven by a weight. The weight hangs on a cord which causes a little pulley wheel to revolve. The pulley wheel has a cam which moves in a slot on the end of the seesaw lever. As the cam revolves it pushes the lever from side to side thus causing the seesaw to tip up and down. The slot is fitted with two lugs which act as stops to the cam.

How quickly the ball runs and the ensuing rate of the seesaw motion depend on the amount of thrust given to the lever. The thrust can be adjusted by resetting the cam. If the lever is 8 inches long (20 cm) the radius of the cam need only be $1/8$ in (3 mm). The driving weight must just be heavy enough to be able to lift the seesaw when the ball is right at one end. If the point of support is screwed fairly tight it will brake the seesaw and prevent it from rattling. A rubber washer will ensure that the braking is even.

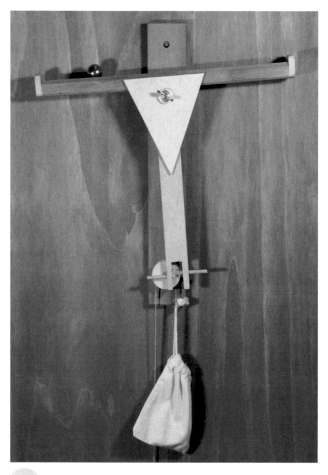

49

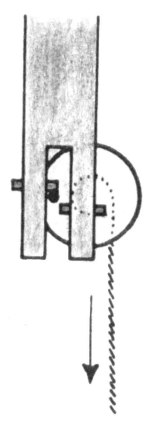

50

Concerning balance

Balancing on a tree trunk, on a wall or even on a tight-rope (which does not need to be all that high off the ground) is an unfailing source of pleasure. By holding a long pole in your hands it is easier to keep your balance, or you can balance the pole on one hand. Keeping your balance when doing a headstand or balancing on the tips of your toes is already the beginning of acrobatics. Also walking on stilts is a matter of balance. All this is playing with gravity. If the opportunity is there children will seize the initiative to experiment with balance.

But even in a small way it is fun playing with gravity. You can build a tower with blocks, higher and higher till it topples over. Then you can start again, building higher and keeping the bottom closer and closer together. You can build the famous house of cards where one outwits the force of gravity.

You can make your own home-made things balance on a point. A suitable point is easily made by sticking a knitting needle into a cork of a bottle. You can balance all kinds of things on a point and make them sway, if their centre of

51

gravity lies below the point. An example is a little man sitting in a boat with an oar at each side. If the man is light enough and the weights heavy enough he will wobble after every little touch, so you expect him to fall (figure 52).

Another suitable motif is a plane. You can hang the weights well below the wings in the engines. The movement appears quite magical.

Another nice toy is shown in figure 54. The top figure, balancing on tiptoes, allows the bottom one to swing gently.

It is possible to ride a bicycle along a rope where the bicycle has no tyres, only the rims of the wheels, and where the handlebars are fixed so that it cannot be steered. Two weights hanging down are fixed rigidly to the bicycle and then it cannot fall (figure 53). This is the same principle as that which I have already described: the centre of gravity must be below the point of support, in this case below the rope.

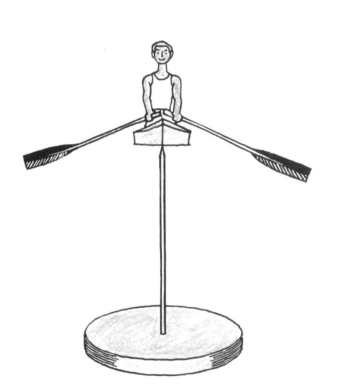

52

53

38

54

Puzzles

Many puzzles are games with or against gravity. Think of the little boxes in which one or several balls can be moved and which you have to get into special holes by moving the box adroitly. You can make such a little box yourself. You don't need glass on the box, but you mustn't cheat, so keep your fingers out of the box! Even in a matchbox you can make cunning little compartments with strips of paper. Put four little balls in it and try to get one ball into each corner.

A variant is the board with slats glued on to it and holes bored in it. The ball must follow a particular course, the slats help it and the holes make it difficult (figure 55). Such things can be bought, and then the board usually has two handles by which it can be moved in the box. This is very interesting, but unnecessary. The board can simply be taken in the hands. You don't even need a box. The balls can be caught in a cloth below. You can then build boards of different difficulty. The edge must always be closed in.

It is also fun to have a maze where the ball does not go along a predetermined course and there are no tricky holes to negotiate, but the lanes can be made narrower and there are dead-ends. You can see who can get the ball to the end quickest.

There is another kind of puzzle which you cannot watch, but which you can listen to. Take a little board, smaller than the one described, and with only one hole for the ball. Stick on closed sides, higher than the ball, and some slats of the same height to make a little maze. Now stick a second board of the same size on top, also with a hole for a ball. Of course, the two holes must not be in line (figure 56). Drop a ball into the top hole and try to move the box in such a way that the ball comes out of the bottom hole. The constructor knows the inside path of the box, but anyone who has not seen him build the maze will have greater difficulty. He can be asked to make a plan of the inside, simply from hearing the ball inside. If that is too easy you can make a second box and stick it under the first. Even a third layer is possible.

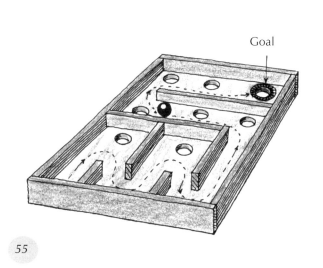

Goal

55

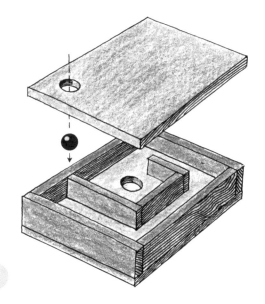

56

40

The sand wheel

Sand runs in an hourglass. But sand, like water, can drive wheels. All the waterwheels described in the second part of this book, 'Playing with Water', can be driven by sand falling from your hand or a funnel. The sand must be dry.

We can develop this further. The sketch in figure 57a shows a little box with one or both sides covered with glass. A sand wheel is set inside it with a funnel over it. A channel leads to the funnel. The sand falls through the opening in the funnel, drives the wheel and falls into a heap at the bottom. When the funnel is empty, turn the box in the direction indicated by the arrow, and the sand will flow back along the channel into the funnel once more, the wheel is 'wound up' again and will start running again. The wheel is made of plywood, and the buckets (or shovels) on the wheel are made of paper. Make the funnel and channel out of stronger paper. The bearings must

be well made and give little friction. The cover can be made of perspex through which holes can be bored. The holes will make good bearings for the axle which is a piece of straight wire. To prevent the wheel slipping sideways set beads as spacers on each side on the axle. The best kind of sand is sand for bird-cages, which you can get in a pet shop.

If you are very cunning you will keep the mechanism a secret by covering the glass leaving only a window for the wheel. The thing becomes even more mysterious if the wheel is also covered and the axle is allowed to protrude and drive something (you can leave the back open to expose the solution to the mystery). You could fix a nimble, light acrobat. How long will it take uninitiated friends to work out how the thing works?

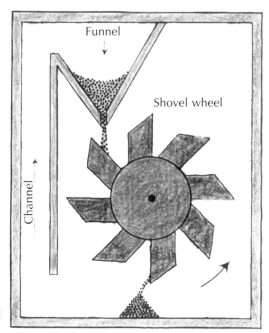

57a

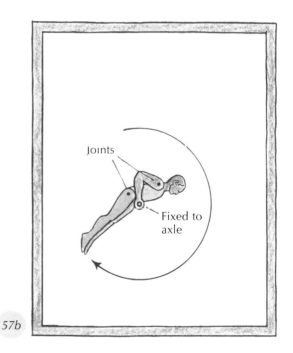

57b

41

58 *Playing with water*

2. Playing with Water

Children first experience the element of water by splashing about in it with their hands and feet. This does not always please adults of course — when children play with water they get wet; that cannot be helped, and the fun is clearly worth it. No real harm is likely to result if they are dried properly afterwards and do not play too long in very cold water. After paddling and splashing about they may start throwing stones into the water to make it splash; to get flat pebbles to skim is more of an art. When children have a bath they like to take all sorts of floating objects in with them. They submerge them and let them shoot up again.

And then there is the fountain! It's very special, with water gushing up day and night, surely something can be done here! A bit more difficult to master is the garden hose, but it is a great attraction and lends itself to all kinds of nonsense. However, the ideal place for playing with water is the babbling brook. It must not be too deep, wide or fast-flowing as to be dangerous; a little harmless brook is best. Round about, there are plenty of things to play with: sand, pebbles, mud, sticks and even bits of wood borne down by the stream. Here children can play for hours without any other toys. You may be surprised to find how many such places still exist, even some with clean water — for pollution usually only occurs lower down once the brook has become a river or a lake, or has flowed into the sea. There is too much water in the sea or a lake for children to do these activities. A stream or brook is safer and the water is gentle enough to be controlled by the children themselves.

After a time even the best game with water and its surroundings has to end. But it can be renewed with a little home-made toy. If you are on holiday with a stream nearby there are all sorts of things you can make. Of course it should be noted that water can be dangerous even where there is only a little of it. Remember that people have fallen so awkwardly that they have drowned in a puddle. Therefore it is recommended that an adult should always supervise water play.

Building dams and channels

Children know instinctively how to play with water. Without adult instigation they will begin to build a dam in a watercourse and make a pond. They break open the dam and with great joy watch the water flooding out. Then they divert the flow into another channel. The water becomes muddy and then clears by itself. It makes interesting swirls and whorls. Little bits of wood float down as boats, the stream has to be changed so that the boats do not get stuck. Harbours are built above and below the works. All too soon evening comes and play has to come to an end, with children dirty, wet and happy.

Once I saw a man in the high mountains playing with icy water in this fashion. When I spoke to this serious-looking gentleman he told me he was just playing; he was on holiday. He was a secondary school teacher. Age is no barrier to the joy of playing with water, thank goodness.

If you cannot easily find such a paradise for playing, something like it can be constructed in the sandpit: water can be brought in a bucket and poured into the channel which the child has made. Occasionally one finds public playgrounds with splendid facilities for creative play, such as a hand pump to pump up water on to a sloping plank, plenty of sand in the sandpit which can be taken to build dams, gutters to catch all the water and lead it on to the next plank, and so on to a third plank. Any of these ideas can be adapted for the smaller sandpit.

Gutters and pipes

Another game with water is to let it flow in wooden gutters. This can be done in any sandpit. A heap of gravel, a partially dried out riverbed, or even a sloping field will also make a good basis. The gutters can be either V-shaped or U-shaped and are made from strips of wood. They should be set up so that they make a proper conduit with little waterfalls. To control the flow, the gradient

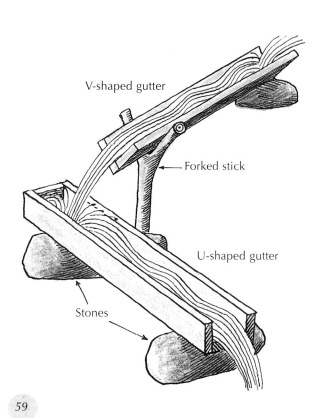

V-shaped gutter

Forked stick

U-shaped gutter

Stones

of the gutters is adjusted by resting them on forked sticks stuck into the ground at the required height, or by using stones as chocks (figure 59). Children will pour water in at the top and enjoy watching it running down along the channels. Adjustments have to be made, and that is all part of the game, as are alterations and extensions. An adult can also make wooden supports to carry the conduit like a marble run or helter-skelter. These should be movable. If the conduit is too fixed the game is limited to pouring water in at the top and watching it, but that is inadequate.

Such conduits were often built in real life. The Romans used stones for building aqueducts whose remains we still admire. Only later did people learn to make pipes by boring out tree trunks; for example, piping spa water. Children can do that too in their play: they can pipe water through a heap of sand, through a 'mountain'. Small pieces of piping are easily available. It does not matter what it is made of; iron, copper, plastic or rubber tubing. Indeed if the pipe is bendable you can make the water flow uphill, once it has gone downhill far enough. The place where it flows out must be lower than the place where it flows in, that is the secret. Civil engineers do this with rivers and call the construction an 'inverted syphon': an upside-down 'bridge' where the road is not taken over the river, but the river is taken under the level road. Civil engineers also build bridges to carry water. Children can do that too (figure 60).

If you are clever you can make water flow uphill first and then downhill, this is called a syphon. You need a piece of tubing. There must be no air-lock in it. It must be completely filled with water. Then the flow is started by sucking at the bottom. Once it has started flowing it will go on flowing until the reservoir at the top end has

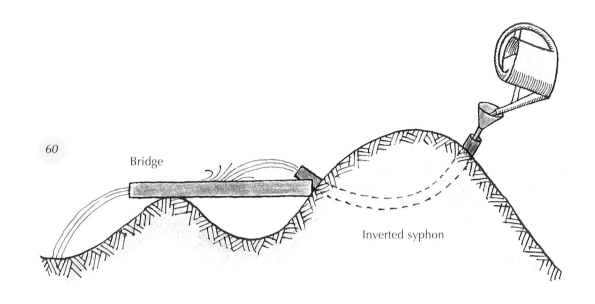

60

Bridge

Inverted syphon

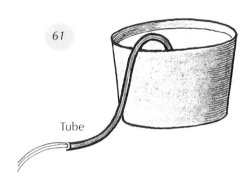

61

Tube

been emptied. In this case too the outflow must lie lower than the inflow (figure 61). Here rainwater can be used if it has been collected in a barrel. There are all sorts of possibilities. Using artificial piping one can also construct waterwheels, and all the wheels turn!

General remarks about waterwheels

If you are going to make a waterwheel you must take the circumstances into consideration, for these can be very diverse. The fall of water can be steep or gentle. Sometimes there is lots of water available, sometimes only a little. You can construct your waterwheel first and then find a suitable water flow.

For water with little fall, that is with a weak current, you need a wheel with large paddles: it will turn slowly, but powerfully. The drive is 'undershot' (that is, the water flows under the wheel). The opposite is a little waterfall, a cascade of water, below which the wheel is set. It gets its power from the greater speed of the water and the drive is 'overshot'. There are all kinds of in-between situations. With a moderate fall the water is taken along channels, not just for fun but to achieve the correct height for the final fall.

You can get the wheel to turn by using a garden hose, but you must ensure that the water drains away properly. Of course with the garden hose one may not be harnessing natural power directly as in many flat places tap water is pumped up mechanically.

It is quite easy to construct a waterwheel. Very simple materials, a little skill and a few tools are required. Do not use glue, but nail, pin and wedge it together. Wood swells in water and so the joints become tight, while glue can sometimes dissolve. A waterwheel which has been allowed to dry out falls to bits quite easily and looks rather derelict. Waterwheels belong in water and should be turning all the time.

The axle of the wheel can lie horizontally, which is the simplest sort, but it can also be vertical, which is harder to build; it is even possible to have the axle lying obliquely. It is important that the wheel should have good bearings. For the horizontal axles you can take a forked branch or suitably shaped stones. Wood does not run so well on wood. It is better to take two different materials, metal and wood or stone. With the vertical axle the bottom of the axle must be pointed and set in a pivot hole. This is called a conical bearing.

I shall now go on to describe examples of waterwheels. Others can be devised. Fortunately waterwheels do not have to be constructed very precisely; they will still work even though they have been clumsily built.

62

63

46

A waterwheel made from a wooden box

As well as the wood from a fruit box you will need an axle. A square shaft of wood is suitable for this, then just nail four similar boards on to the sides of the square shaft and hammer in a larger nail at each end as an extension to the axle. For bearings, take suitably forked sticks and drive them into the bed of the stream. Set this simple wheel deep enough to let the current flow undershot and drive the boards round. Another way is to bring a jet of water overshot on to the wheel, in which case the boards should not touch the water below. In the first case the wheel will turn slowly, but in the second it will turn quickly. In either case the wheel needs starting otherwise it can stick midway when no water is catching the boards. This wheel can be built in various

sizes. The longer the boards the more strongly the wheel will work, because the length increases the leverage. Similarly, wide boards catch more water and so increase the power of the wheel.

More boards also increase the power and ensure that the wheel turns smoothly. By planing the edges of the square wooden axle an octagonal piece is formed which makes it possible to build a better wheel, but then there is the difficulty of nailing on the boards, especially the last one. In this case split the axle in half or even in quarters, nail the boards on and then tie it together again.

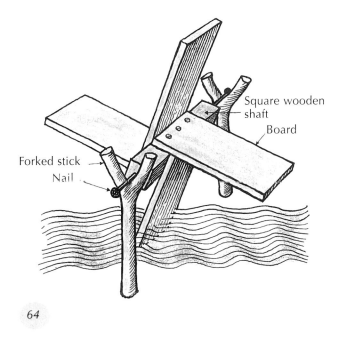

Square wooden shaft
Board
Forked stick
Nail

64

65

A waterwheel made of forked twigs

Select at least eight forked sticks with long straight stems. Fix at least six of them into a hub, and use the last two as a bearing. Willow or alder, found growing beside water, are suitable. Both kinds of tree soon grow again so one does no real damage by cutting wands from them. Of course in a conservation area one cannot take them. The size of the wheel can be anything from an inch to 3 feet (2 cm to 1 m) in diameter, that is, with forked twigs up to 18 inches (50 cm) long.

The hub is a thick log with regularly spaced slits cut in it to take the sharpened forks. For bigger wheels, bore holes instead of cutting slits. For paddles, fix boards or pieces of tin to the forked ends. Leaves or even paper will do for small wheels. The finished wheel should be reasonably balanced, and this should be taken into consideration during construction. Push the last two sticks upright into the bed of the stream as bearings. Drive nails into the ends of the axle to run in the bearings or simply taper the axle at the ends (figure 66).

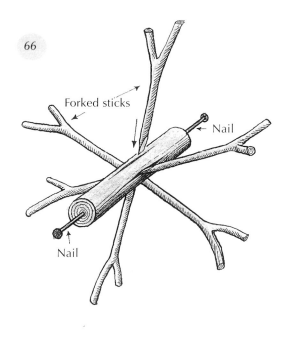

66

Forked sticks

Nail

Nail

67

A wheel of bowls

Water makes particularly beautiful patterns when falling into a vessel. You can fix bowls to an axle. These bowls can be carved out or you can use walnut shells for a small wheel. The problem is how to fix them. The best way is to split willow wands and bore holes in the nutshells. Then tie the nutshells on to the wands (figure 69). Stick the willow rods into a hub made from a log as described in the last model. Of course you can also use discs with holes in them as a hub. These can be bought in a model shop.

To drive this kind of wheel a thin jet of water is most suitable. Any tap will give this jet, but it is more fun to make a channel outside as has already been described.

The full-sized wheel is called a 'pelton wheel'. It is made of metal, is 3 feet (1 m) or more thick and is driven by a jet as thick as your arm coming from a high reservoir. Unfortunately you cannot watch it in operation as the wheel is enclosed for safety. But with our kind of wheel you can watch it — for hours on end.

Similar wheels, only bigger and with an upright axle, are still to be found, for instance, in the Balkans (figure 68). A fairly thin cascade flows against quarter bowls and drives them round. Such a wheel can be copied. The jet has to fall at an angle.

68   *Spoon-wheel of a mill from Romania, 1850*

Bore 4 holes in the nutshell

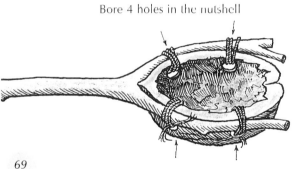

69

49

A wheel with cones

You can also construct a waterwheel using thick paper. Start with a wooden wheel, which can be taken from an old toy, for instance. Make paper cones and fasten them on to the wheel with drawing pins. Of course this kind of wheel will not take too strong a cascade, nor will it go on working indefinitely, but it will run merrily for a time. If you have tin-snips and the necessary skill you can make the cones from old tins, even soldering them. Then nail the cones on to the rim of the wheel. Such a wheel will last until the axle wears out (figure 70).

A waterwheel with compartments

Once the basic principles are understood, it is not really any more difficult to build a larger waterwheel. As models, we can take the real-life wheels which can still be seen in operation in places such as the Southern Tyrol. The greatest problem is making the wall segments of the wheel. These must be cut out from thin boards. Such boards can be obtained from do-it-yourself shops. The ring segments should have an inside radius of about 6 inches (15 cm). Draw the segments on the wood with a pair of compasses.

Axle

Fixed cones

70

72   The waterwheel in use

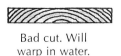

Bad cut. Will warp in water.

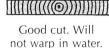

Good cut. Will not warp in water.

71

If the compasses will not stretch to the required radius you can use a piece of string. One end is tied to a nail at the centre of the circle. A pencil is tied to the other end of the string. The segments are then cut out with a fretsaw or a bandsaw. The number of segments depends on the width of the boards from which they are cut. You will need at least four, but wheels can also be built with more. If you want to do the job professionally the segments will be joined together by tongue and groove, but it is perfectly adequate to join them together by nailing little boards on to them outside (figure 73). I would recommend zinc nails for this task and for the subsequent joinery.

The two rings must of course be the same size. Between these fix the compartment walls at regular intervals. They must be set at an angle so that the water does not spill out too soon.

The compartments are now closed at the back by boards inside the two rings. You can also make the compartment walls so long that they form the bottom of the next compartment (figure 74).

Fix four 'spokes' right across the wheel in the form of a cross leaving a space in the middle for the axle (figure 75). The axle beam is square and fixed to the wheel by four wedges on each side. This is also done on life-size wheels. This allows the wheel to be set properly and to be removed for repair, and is a very practical arrangement. Thick nails in the axle beam form the running axle. Of course you can bore a hole in the axle beam and use screws instead of nails.

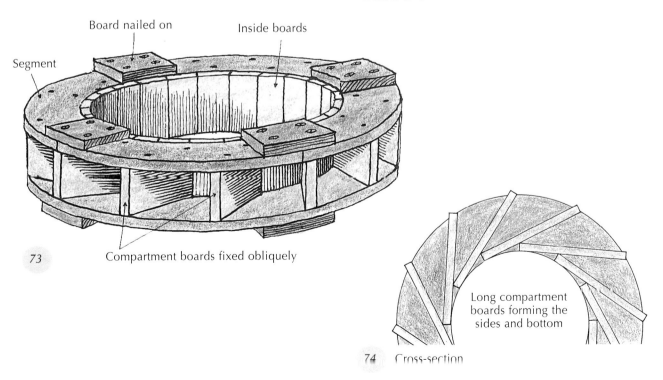

Board nailed on

Inside boards

Segment

73   Compartment boards fixed obliquely

Long compartment boards forming the sides and bottom

74   Cross-section

Once the wheel is ready it is necessary to construct a mounting for the bearing. Conditions can be so diverse that it is impossible to give any general instructions. Notches cut in two cross beams are sufficient to make a bearing, but how the cross beams are held up is left to you.

Such a massive wheel requires a powerful cascade falling into its compartments. You may be lucky to find a little natural waterfall under which the wheel fits, but usually conditions are not so suitable and you will have to build ducts as described at the beginning of the book. The gutters must be supported so that they bring about the necessary fall. This waterwheel works best overshot; that is, with the water coming on to it from above, and the wheel is driven by the weight of the falling water. Such a wheel has power. It should drive something.

Making waterwheels work things

Once you have built a waterwheel and got it working you will want to make it drive something. There are all kinds of possibilities, for instance, a power hammer (figure 78), or a small figure as in (figure 76). You can get the wheel to drive a doll's roundabout and give someone's dolls a ride, or it can drive a great wheel or a cable railway. Fast-turning wheels can drive a bicycle dynamo which in turn can light a lamp. You can obtain the necessary speed for the dynamo by 'step-up conversion'; that is, by getting a large wheel to drive a small one. You can take a bicycle wheel and fix it to the waterwheel. The bicycle wheel now drives a belt or cord (in the rim) round a smaller rimmed wheel. Unfortunately, it is not easy to obtain a small rimmed wheel in model shops. The little wheel revolves more quickly but it has less power. A 'step-down conversion' with

75

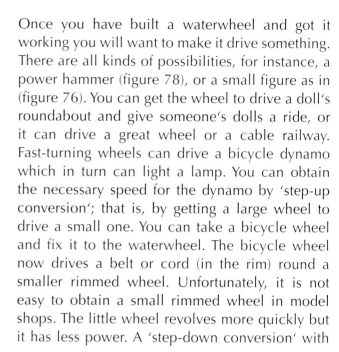

76

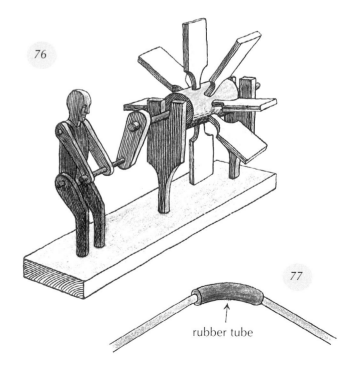

77

rubber tube

more power but less speed is when a little wheel drives a larger one. If the cord or belt slips in the rim, rubber bands can be fixed in the rims. Another way is to prolong the axle by joining it to a shaft. A rubber tube over the end of the axle and over the end of the shaft makes the join. The shaft then drives the device. The advantage is that there is no cord to slip. The disadvantage is that there is no gearing in the transmission.

Once the wheel has been coupled up to the plaything, you can regulate it so that it goes faster or slower or stops altogether. This is done by regulating the flow of water by a sluice. If you can do that you are a master waterworks builder.

Waterwheels can also be set on little boats. If these are anchored or moored in a river the current drives the wheels. There are still mills in the lower Danube which operate in this way. To copy these, all you need is a board on which two bearings are mounted. Lay the axle across and fix two waterwheels, one at each end. A cam fixed to the axle can be made to drive hammers. Then in the stream it hammers away as if dwarfs or water spirits were at work ...

Figure 78 shows such a hammer without the boat. The base carries the mountings for the two hammers and the bearings for the axle of the wheel. The wheel carries pegs to lift the hammer shafts. The contraption can only revolve in one direction (clockwise on the photograph). In this case the wheel is turned by a cord running to the waterwheel.

78

79

Figures 78 and 79. A waterwheel driving a power hammer and a merry-go-round!

Bucket wheels

In playing with water we must not omit the bucket wheel, an ancient invention. In real life they are used in irrigation. They are driven by flowing water to lift a small amount of the stream to a higher level. Some of these wheels can still be seen usually preserved as historical monuments, for instance in Bavaria, Germany (figure 81).

With a little patience you can also build models. At regular intervals fix some containers on to the circumference of a wheel with a horizontal axle. Then take either little clay pots or pieces of bamboo cane, cut so that a knot forms the bottom of each container. The wheel is undershot by a stream that is not flowing too fast. The containers dip into the water, are lifted out full and empty themselves when they reach the top. You can either let the water pour down again freely and enjoy the cascade, or catch it in a tank with a gutter leading out of it. Watching the water and the forms which it makes is an important part of water play.

The bucket wheel does not need to be as complicated as the one in the photo. For example, the wheel in figure 70 can be developed by using the cones as water containers and by adding paddles to drive the wheel. Also the wheel in figure 75 can be modified to make a bucket wheel by fitting containers to the outside. Of course, this latter wheel will be undershot.

80   On the way to the water

81   A Franconian bucket-wheel

Underwater wheels

You can also make an underwater 'windmill' like a ship's propeller in reverse. Take a square block of wood. Cut an oblique groove on each of four faces and fix a thin board or sheet of tin in each. Use a nail as an axle, a bead as a spacer and a thick stick driven into the bed of the stream as a bearing. By using a rimmed wheel and a cord you can transmit the power of the water and drive something.

In real life this contraption is used for measuring the speed of the current, for instance, in a water main. The propeller is protected by a pipe. On a much larger scale a strong propeller with a vertical axle is set in a large pipe. Whole rivers are funnelled into the pipe. This device is called a 'Kaplan turbine' after its Austrian inventor.

The 'snipe'

Nowadays, the 'snipe' (figure 84) is less well known than the waterwheel. In former times, in the mountainous regions of Central Europe, the snipe worked as an automatic hammer in the forges. Today, you can occasionally see it set up in a museum where it operates with a regular rhythm. The principle is very simple and easily understood: a container is fastened to one end of a seesaw into which water flows until there is enough to make the seesaw tip and the container empties. A counterweight on the other end of the seesaw ensures that it comes back up to the horizontal, and the whole process starts all over again. The snipe must be well-balanced in order to function properly. Make the water container by nailing some boards together. A stone can

Pulley wheel
with spacer
bead behind

Nail as axle

Square block of wood

Alternative
assembly

82

be used as a hammer weight. The seesaw dips through an angle of 90° and is prevented from dipping further by a buffer (figure 83). After some adjustments the snipe will function every bit as well as a waterwheel and tap, tap, tap, it goes. You can make it any size, even very small with a nutshell as water-container.

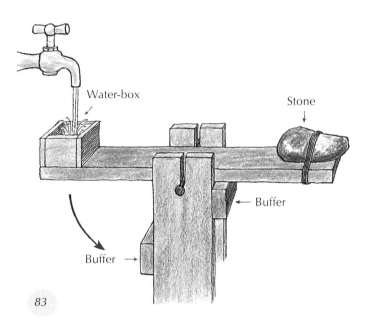

83

84

Hydraulic power transmission

With a plastic surgical syringe not only can children squirt water all over the place and annoy nice people but can also create a hydraulic transmission as used in every car brake, as well as in bulldozers and excavators. In addition to two syringes without needles, you need a long piece of valve tubing which you can buy in cycle shops. One syringe is filled with water. The tube is fitted to the end of the syringe and filled with water by pressing the syringe. On the other end fix the second syringe half filled. Between the two pistons, inside the cylinders and in the tube there must be only water, no air bubbles (figure 85). When one syringe is pressed in, the other one goes out, and vice versa: hydraulic transmission. If you have two syringes of different sizes the whole thing becomes more exciting: the smaller piston moves more quickly, but has less power and the larger piston moves more slowly but with more power: ratio transmission. Because the tube is long and adaptable, unlike cog-wheel, belt or rod transmission, surprising effects can be achieved. All that is needed is a bit of imagination!

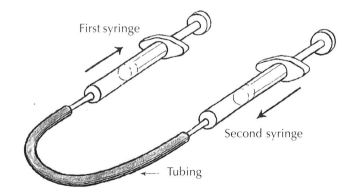

85

56

Submarines and fish

Some things float in water and some sink. But it is possible to create an in-between condition: an object that is in a buoyant state. Fishes are naturally created in this way, so that they can maintain their buoyancy in water. Submarines are built on the same principle. There are various ways of achieving this buoyant condition. You can saw out a wooden fish. In order that it does not just lie on its side in the water, fix a staple underneath. The staple must be right in the middle. It will probably not be heavy enough to suspend the fish until you hang pieces of bent wire from the staple so that the fish really does remain suspended (figure 86). You can also get any watertight bottle to remain bouyant. Fill it with just enough water so that it neither rises to the surface nor sinks to the bottom. Much patience is needed for this bath-time game.

The water demon

By putting a medicine bottle upside-down into a glass jar filled to the brim with water we can make it rise and sink. The medicine bottle should still have the dropper on it and be filled with so much water that it is just suspended. If you now press the water in the jar with the flat of your hand (the hand must cover the mouth of the jar completely) you compress the air in the bottle, the water fills the space and the bottle sinks. You can also cover the jar with clingfilm, then you won't get your hands wet. The clingfilm shuts the cylinder like the cellophane on a jar of preserves. Tie it on tightly. There must be no air underneath. The cover must lie flush on the water. In former times instead of the medicine bottle people in Central Europe used a hollow glass called a 'water demon', hence the name. You can also paint the bottle in this way and make your demon rise and sink, or keep it suspended in the middle (figure 87) .

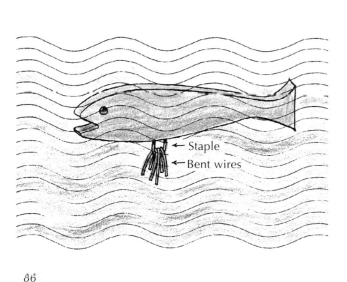

← Staple
← Bent wires

86

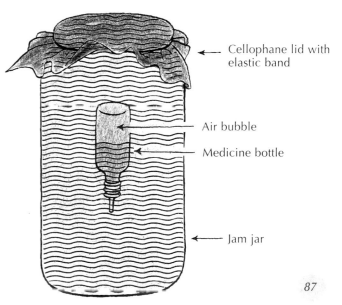

← Cellophane lid with elastic band

Air bubble

Medicine bottle

← Jam jar

87

The diver

Fix a stone to a balloon and attach a thin rubber tube to the mouth of the balloon. This makes a little diver. Blow into the tube, the balloon expands and rises. Let some air out and the stone makes the balloon sink. It's surprising how big a stone the balloon can lift in water (figure 88).

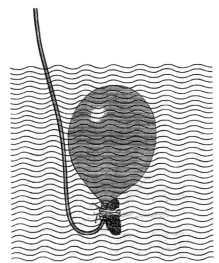

88

The ferry

Over a reasonably wide brook a ferry can be rigged up. Stretch a cord with a pulley wheel on it across the stream. The pulley wheel runs on an axle which is bent round to form an eye (figure 89). The eye must be heavy enough to hang down under its own weight. Next, construct the ferry which can be in the form of a narrow raft. Screw in an eye to each side of the raft about a third of the way from the end. Tie a string to the eye on the pulley and tie a hook on the other end of the string. Attach the hook to the eye on the side of the raft nearest the bank. Launch the raft and the current will drive the raft over to the other side of the brook as the raft lies at an angle to the current. Once the raft has reached the other side unhook the string and hook it on to the other eye and the ferry will return to its starting place. Now a harbour can be built on each side of the stream and freight and doll passengers can be ferried across.

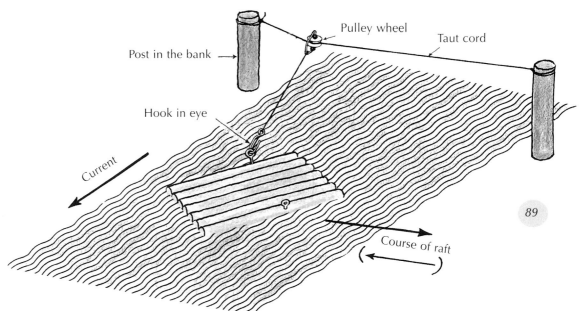

Post in the bank

Pulley wheel

Taut cord

Hook in eye

Current

Course of raft

89

Little boats

I have already said so much about playing with water, and yet have not mentioned a very obvious ploy: playing with boats. I must emphasize that I shall not describe building model boats, for there are plenty of books and plans already. Exact scale model boats that do not float are fine ornaments for a room but do not have a place in water play. In the same way, floating models with remote controls do not really constitute play with water.

Playing with boats begins when children throw bits of bark or wood into a stream and run along beside them until the bits get caught in the bank. Then with a stick the ship is freed and the voyage continues. Next, the course of the stream is altered so that the little boat no longer gets stuck at the sides, and then playing with the water is underway.

Now we can move from the unformed piece of wood to all kinds of boats, but to enjoy making them it is necessary to know a few fundamental laws.

A boat must float properly and where possible it should have a little doll as crew and where that is the case it must not capsize! You should, therefore, build flat. A flat board floats with more stability while a log easily turns over — it is unstable. That is to say: board-like boats keep their balance, but log-like boats, however elegantly formed, tip over easily. To prevent capsizing, the boat can be weighted underneath, but in order to compensate for this weight you must make the boat lighter or it will sink, even though it is made of wood. Hollow out the boat, and for best results cover it with a watertight deck. To carve a boat symmetrically is not so easy. Home-made carved-out boats usually sail in a circle; but this can be counteracted by a rudder. A further step is building ribs covered with strakes, but here we are in the realm of model building which is beyond the scope of this book.

It is better if you do not try to copy real boats but build according to this basic law: flat-building without a heavy keel. Even though it is easy to carve a dugout, you will not get much joy out of it without an outrigger, such as is used, for instance, by the South Sea islanders (figure 90). From this, move to two equal bodies joined together, the catamaran. These boats maintain their balance so well that they can carry a sail (see also Sailing boats, p. 99).

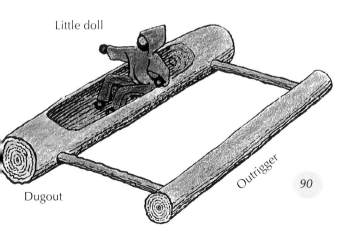

Little doll

Dugout

Outrigger

90

A paddle steamer

For windless days or for playing in the bath you can build a paddle steamer driven by elastic. Now natural materials are not sufficient, you must do some modelling at home. With a fretsaw cut out a board in the form of a ship (figure 91): pointed at the prow, square at the stern, and inside, a rectangular hole. Saw out two boards in a rectangular form somewhat smaller than the piece cut out of the waist of the boat. Cut a slot in each of the boards so that they can be fitted together in the form of a cross. This cross makes the paddle wheel that will drive the steamer forward. Fasten two elastic bands round the paddle and attach them to two pins at the side of the boat (figure 91). Now wind up this 'Mississippi paddle steamer'. With luck and good construction the ship will travel for a few yards. By fitting a rudder, for instance, a piece of bendable tin, you can make your vessel travel in a curve or circle. Notice the waves which this little boat sets up when it goes over calm water. If it is big enough it can carry a doll.

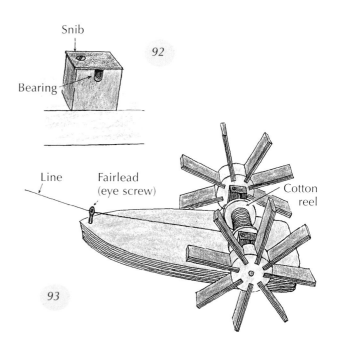

92

Snib

Bearing

Line   Fairlead
(eye screw)

Cotton reel

93

94

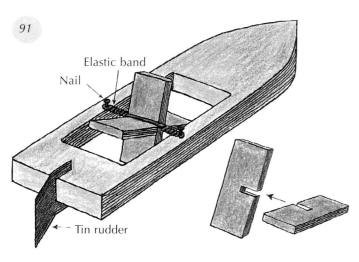

91

Elastic band

Nail

Tin rudder

A boat to sail against the current

We have already used water power to turn waterwheels. Under certain conditions it is also possible to use water power to drive a ship against the current. The boat, however, must be attached to a cord by which it can wind itself upstream. The cord winds on to a windlass on board the boat. The windlass is turned by two paddle wheels driven by the current. The diameter of the paddle wheels must be quite a bit bigger than that of the windlass; the principle being a matter of leverage (figure 93).

Start by taking a board of light wood, fir or pine, cut into the shape of a boat. Take an ordinary cotton reel and put it on an axle. The reel and the axle now require a mounting on the board. One way of doing this is shown on figure 92. Fix the axle on the mounting, and bolt it in so that it cannot jump out of the bearing. Make two octagonal hubs with slots sawn in. Fix thin boards (of sufficient length!) into the slots and fix to each end of the axle. Now for the cord. The best is nylon line, because it does not absorb water. Fix one end of the line securely on to the windlass and then wind on about 30 feet (10 m). Thread the other end of the line through a fairlead (the fairlead can be a staple or an eye screw) at the bow of the boat. Now the fun can start. Unwind the line and let the boat drift downstream. Hold on to the end of the line. When the line comes taut the boat will start winding up the line on to the windlass and so paddle its way back to you. You can keep it in the middle of the current by the line (figure 94).

A balloon boat

Water and air can play together in this little boat that is driven by a balloon (figure 95). Tie a straw or tube to the balloon, blow it up and the escaping air will propel the boat forwards with a great bubbling of water. Unfortunately it won't go very far.

95

A water rocket

Fix a rubber tube into the screw top of a large (1 litre/quart) plastic bottle. Bend the tube over and clamp it shut with a clothes peg. Fix a bicycle valve into the bottom of the bottle. Half fill the bottle with water, and then start pumping in air with a bicycle pump. The pressure rises in the bottle. Stop before it bursts. For a launching ramp use a laboratory clamp or a board with a notch cut out (figure 96). Put the bottle with the tube below, and then as quickly as possible release the clothes peg. The air pressure forces the water out and the rocket rises. It is best to try this outside with swimwear to avoid the fun being spoilt.

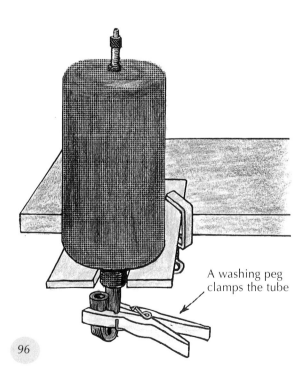

A washing peg clamps the tube

96

Floating stones

Of course there are stones that float: pumice floats. However, here's a game which can be made from simple odds and ends.

First we need a collection of different sized pebbles from pea-sized to plum-sized. Then float a flat empty tin in a bowl of water. (We may also each need a tablemat to protect the table.)

Each player takes a stone from the pile in the centre. It is best to begin by taking the smallest. The player who takes the last stone begins by placing one stone in the floating tin. Now it is best to start with the biggest stone. Each player in turn adds another stone into the 'boat'. Soon we reach the critical stage when adding another stone sinks the boat. The player who added the fateful stone has to take all the stones from the bowl and can immediately begin a new round. The player who first has no stones left is the winner.

Of course no one may touch the boat or shake the table.

You can, of course, make a stone that floats. Take a crumpled paper ball and cover it with clay, making sure it is closed and smooth all over. Then ask a potter to fire and glaze the clay 'stone.' The paper turns to ash leaving a hollow space inside, and the stone floats! See how many people you can fool with this stone.

97

Water   Tin with stones

Bowl

A vortex

Everyone has seen a vortex as the water drains out of the bath. But you can catch a different view of this amazing phenomenon using a plastic bottle. Carefully cut off the base of the bottle and drill a hole through the lid (figure 99a). Fill the upside-down bottle with warm water keeping a finger on the hole in the lid. Stir the water until a vortex forms (figure 99b) and then open the hole. Gently shaking the bottle will make the vortex bend like a snake. Adding a few drops of ink or paint will colour the water and make it more beautiful.

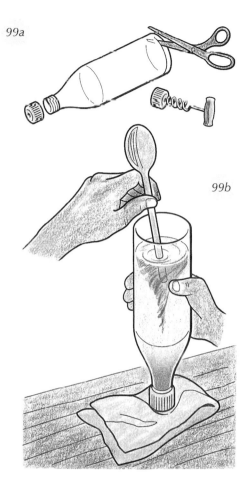

99a

99b

98

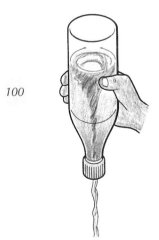

100

The colour of water

What is the colour of water? If we look at a glass of water, the answer is obvious: it is clear and has no colour. But if we look around us in nature, streams, pools, lakes, rivers or the sea can be blue, turquoise, green, grey, brown, ochre. All kinds of things have an effect on the colour: suspended particles, lighting, the colour of the bottom, reflections.

When I go on walks I carry a little mirror with me. I often stop at a bank of water and immerse the mirror, holding it so that I see neither the bottom nor the sky. The mirror then shows a uniform colour that is surprisingly varied in different waters.

101   Three lakes in the Engadine, Switzerland

A game of skill and patience

Steel does not float. Pins are made of steel, therefore they will not float. Or will they? If you have a steady hand, try this.

Lay a pin on top of water in a teacup (using tweezers may help). Water has a very thin skin which can support small objects. There are insects which make use of this to walk on the surface of ponds (figure 102). The skin (or surface tension) of the water also holds a drop of water together (figure 103).

102

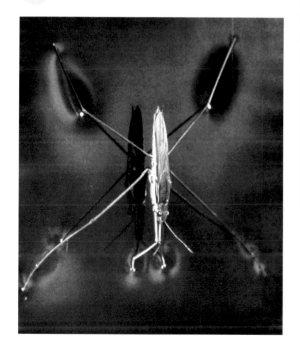

103

3. Playing with Fire

An adult must always be present when playing around a fire. Before lighting a fire in the open, check whether it's allowed. Never leave a fire unattended, and when finished make sure it's completely extinguished.

Although I hope it is obvious that 'playing with fire' is not meant literally, still the title of this part is rather startling. Of course matches are not available for children to play with, but quite rightly they like imitating. When they see an adult lighting a match, they want to try out this marvellous work of art. And then the accident happens.

At the right age every child has to learn how to use a match, how to control fire. The most natural way, as with all learning, is in play under a grown-up's supervision. The child who has been introduced carefully to this element will know its potential and its power and will treat it with due caution. Here I shall try to show how such a careful acquaintance with the most dangerous of the four elements can be made.

By playing with fire I mean playing with its effects, with warmth and light, not just kindling a fire. Again such contrivances have been selected in which something is driven by the power of fire or which produces remarkable effects. Here little fires with the flames only big enough to meet the object of the exercise are best. The fire is guarded and kept under control. A sensible treatment of the elements is practised.

104 Jumping over a fire

Iron smelting *105*

First one should take the opportunity of showing the child little fires, acquainting them with the candle flame. In many families a candle is lit for festive occasions. Having meals with a lit candle heightens the sense of ceremony. Evening prayers are said by candlelight. Birthdays, Advent and Christmas are celebrated in candlelight. In these customs fire is made sacred and reverence is engendered.

If you use solid fuel for heating, the child will have a direct experience of the heat and light of fire. The sight of the flame of the oil or gas burner in a domestic central-heating system is possible without danger.

If you manage to visit a furnace you will be impressed with the sight through the inspection hole in the furnace. It is hard to visit an iron-smelting works, especially with children. That is understandable, but it is a pity. On the other hand glass-blowers usually encourage visitors, and that can be an impressive experience seeing

the glowing glass ready to be shaped. A smithy with an open coal fire is rare nowadays. If you do have the chance, take your child and they will no doubt watch the smith patiently for hours on end. There are also miniature and full-size railways where it is possible to experience the power of the steam engine and its fire. These different forms of technology should help develop the necessary respect for fire.

In many parts of Central Europe fire wheels are rolled down the mountain at Easter, and at the summer solstice fires are lit on the mountain tops and in the valleys. Children are allowed to stay up longer on these occasions. They are allowed to take out burning brands and make glowing circles and figures of eight in the night air, although naturally the adults are fully attentive to dangerous possibilities. Similarly, bigger children jump over the fire; here one must be aware that clothing made of artificial fibres can be dangerous.

Picnics are a good opportunity to make a fire with the little ones and roast sausages, apples and potatoes in the embers. Aspiring scouts can attempt to light the fire without paper as a point of honour, and can cook whole menus in the open air.

106   A blacksmith at work

Midsummer fire   107

For children you can build a little oven and cook some soup (figure 108). It's even simpler to fry an egg in a small frying pan over an open fire (figure 109). You can also contain the fire in a clay bowl (figure 110). These can also be bought, and the inventors write, 'It's wonderful to watch children intently observing the flames, adding twigs and experiencing the warmth. Even the most restless child becomes quiet and contemplative.' (www.denk-keramik.de).

At Martinmas, in some countries, in the early November evening children are taken on a lantern procession, singing at the same time. The lanterns are made at home using stiff card. On New Year's Eve there is a continental tradition of going for a walk through the deep snow of the winter forest with burning torches. Children are allowed to carry burning torches as well (wearing old gloves, as the pitch from the torches is inclined to dribble down). In the darkness the torches create a kind of illuminated space which travels with each participant. It is planned so that at midnight the processions converge in an open clearing.

And then of course there are the fireworks of Guy Fawkes or July 4th when some quite spectacular effects of fire can be seen.

108

109

110

111

Torches in a cave

Martinmas lantern

Take a balloon, blow it up and tie a knot. Stick layers of coloured tissue paper on the balloon with wallpaper paste, beginning at the rounded end of the balloon (not the end with the knot). Carry on adding paper until you're past the middle of the balloon. Paste a string to either side of what will be the opening. Now wait a few hours until the paste has dried out. Then let the air out of the balloon, carefully prising it from the tissue paper. Using your string, hang the lantern with wire from a stick, and put a night light (tea light) inside. It can help to glue the night light to the lantern.

Lamps for the garden

A Martinmas lantern can of course be used as a garden lamp, but you can also make a standing lamp. Tie sticks together as shown in figure 112, and cover with white or coloured translucent paper, like tissue paper, kite paper or Japanese Washi (Wagami) paper, leaving an opening at the top. Put one or several nightlights on to a small flat surface inside. The lamps look lovely at night. You can also make them square, five or six-sided. But remember these lamps aren't rain proof!

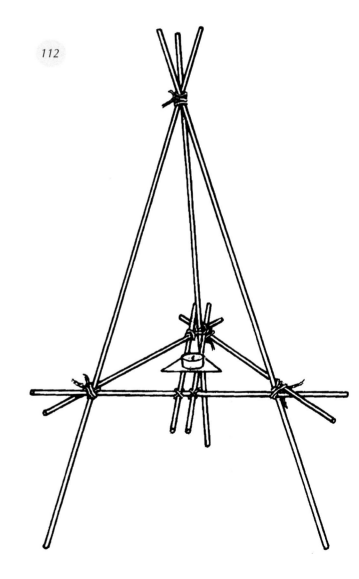

112

70

Experiments with candle flame

The great scientist Michael Faraday can teach us much about the versatility of the ordinary candle flame. His Lectures on the Chemical History of a Candle were addressed to young people. Some of the following experiments are taken from his suggestions.

Children love to see how flames spurt out when we squeeze orange peel at a candle flame. It happens because the etheric oils ignite spontaneously in little cross flames, visible only for a moment, before vanishing. Again we squirt and again the little firework appears and vanishes.

You can show children where the flame is at its hottest by holding the head of a match for a moment right in the middle of the candle flame before it ignites, whereas you cannot hold it at the edge or immediately above without it lighting at once. If you hold a matchstick straight through the flame for a short time it will show two brand marks from the edge of the flame but nothing in the middle.

Light a second candle and blow the first one out. 'Smoke' rises. After a few moments hold the still burning candle in the rising gases just above the wick (see figure 113); a flame will spring down on to the extinguished wick and the candle, which has just been blown out, lights again. The springing of the flame happens as quickly as lightning — you hardly believe you saw it. Try it again. See how far the flame will jump. Finally it becomes obvious that hot candle gases burn.

These gases shine palely. This phenomenon can be observed in dim light. It is difficult to catch sight of this pale light because one's eyes need to be accustomed to the dark but are still under the influence of burning candle. However, if you are curious enough you will find a way of seeing this mysterious incandescence.

113

114

If you let a little piece of golden or silver decorating wax dissolve in the pool of molten wax in the candle under the flame, it will show what is happening in the liquid wax: there is a constant spiralling in the middle as the wax is drawn up into the wick. The spiralling on the surface goes outwards, down at the edge and then towards the wick. In the decorating wax there are minute particles of metal which show up these currents (figure 114).

It is quite simple and well worth the effort to create the shadow of a candle flame. Shine an incandescent lamp, or better still the lamp of a projector, on to a lit candle. On the wall behind you will be able to see the black shadow of the candle and the wick, while the flame appears as light grey with a bright edge, while above it veils like delicate curtains move; that is the warm air rising (figure 115). You can also blow, or wave your hands and then you will see whirls for a short time.

115

Leidenfrost

Johann Leidenfrost was a physician in the eighteenth century. He first described an odd phenomenon. Despite his name it has nothing to do with frost — quite the opposite. If you spill some water on a hot plate, the drops will dance about, moving very quickly until they evaporate. Try it out when you have a chance, but watch you don't touch the hot plate!

Party lights

Cut a house out of card then cut out lots of windows — big ones, little ones, square ones, round ones. When it gets dark, put some nightlights behind to make special lighting. If you want to do a really good job, stick coloured tissue paper over the windows and add a few mirrors. You can make a whole street scene like that.

The same method can be used for coloured transparencies at Christmas or for Advent calendars.

116

The spiral

The first and simplest 'warmth-machine' is the gyrating spiral. It does not drive anything, but it gyrates in the warm rising air of a radiator. It is quite simple to make. Take a piece of paper about 8 inches (20 cm) square, rather stronger than writing paper. On this draw a good even spiral freehand. When you have managed to produce a good drawing, cut it out and it will undo itself hanging down. Push a press stud into the middle of the spiral with the hollow part downwards. This is the bearing. Now place the spiral resting on a knitting needle, so that it can revolve freely on it (see figure 118). After that you have only to make the base for the needle which you do by boring a hole in a little board and inserting the needle. Put it on a radiator or a closed stove and it will turn as long as the radiator is warm, right through the winter. The bottom end of the spiral is inclined to curl up. Bend it down otherwise it will act as a brake in the hot-air current.

 117

 118   Press stud as bearing

119

The hot-air roundabout

Warm air rising from a candle can be used to drive something like a little dolls' roundabout. For this to function properly I must explain the principle.

The most important thing is the bearing. It must allow very easy movement. Here again we can use the press-stud bearing already mentioned, but another kind of bearing is better: the conical bearing where the needle rests in a small round tin ($^1/6$ in, 4 mm diameter). You can obtain such a tin at an electrical supplier or modelling shop. The tins have a thread on the outside so that they can be fixed easily. A hub carries the blades that produce the rotation, but the centre of gravity of the rotor must be below the bearing. That means that the tin must project above the hub (see figure 119).

The blades are made out of thin wood or tin. Everything that turns must be lightly built, in order to minimize the friction on the bearing. The blades require very little pitch; best if they can be made adjustable, with round pegs fitting into holes in the hub. Tin can be bent and so is more easily adjusted. By trial and error you will find the best pitch.

As with the spiral the needle can be set in a base. Of course you can also just use a pin stuck in a nicely formed shaft. To try the roundabout out place it on a radiator. Once it is turning properly you can tie threads on to the ends of the blades from which are suspended little boards on which you can place little light dolls. These then rotate. In my house such a roundabout once stood on the radiator and the dolls went round all winter, day and night.

Of course you can make the roundabout revolve by placing lighted candles underneath but then great caution is required.

Here is another suggestion for this construction. Make a tripod out of wire (see figure 120). It has a nail on top. On this nail set a concave metal disc (with no sharp edge) as a kind of hat, which you can cut out from thin non-combustible metal foil. It has flaps through which the rising warm air turns the hat. Place a lighted candle beneath and the little roundabout will begin to turn. On the outside stick some pieces of the same material and bend them down to make seats. On these you can let little light dolls ride.

This principle is also used in the Christmas angel chimes, or in the beautiful wooden Christmas pyramid of the Erzgebirge.

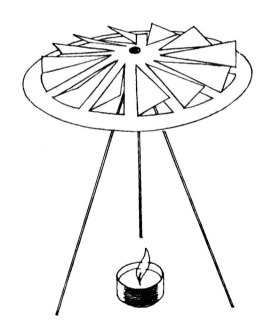

120

The shadow roundabout

The shadow roundabout is a variation of the roundabout. It is constructed in much the same way as the one already described. It is driven by one candle only and for pendants you can cut out people, animals, and so on, from thin card (figure 121). Round the outside stretch some tracing paper which will catch the shadows of the figures as they revolve. It is also nice to stick cut-outs on to the tracing paper, but these should be of immobile objects such as trees, flowers, hedges and houses. Now the figures will move as shadows among these things. A particularly suitable motif for a Christmas shadow-play is the 'Flight into Egypt'.

For the rotating blades of this model thin tin is recommended. The tracing paper should not reach right down to the bottom otherwise the candle inside will not get any fresh air.

A subsidiary effect of these candle-driven roundabouts is the play of light and shadow on the ceiling.

122   The finished shadow roundabout

123   The roundabout when lit

121   Inside the shadow roundabout

The hot-air balloon

You can make a hot-air balloon yourself. It is not too difficult but it takes a long time and it is a unique experience once the balloon rises filled with hot air. It is no ploy for little children.

The material for the balloon is ordinary tissue paper, colour according to choice — balloons of two different colours are especially nice. There are six segments making up the balloon. You need to have twelve sheets of tissue paper. The sheets are glued together in pairs along the short edge. I recommend that you make a stencil out of newspaper or large wrapping paper according to figure 124. (This ensures similarly shaped segments, and saves a lot of preparation if your balloon should go up in flames.) The figure is based on the commonly available tissue paper size of 20 x 30 inches (50 x 76 cm). If your tissue paper is a different size adjust the stencil proportionally. Fold the pairs of tissue paper (now 20 x 60 inches, 50 x 150 cm) lengthwise. As the segments are symmetrical the paper can be cut double. Make a fold along the curved edge about $1/2$ inch (1 cm) wide. When the six segments have been cut stick them together at the folds according to figure 125. When the last fold is stuck to the first strip the balloon is almost finished. All it now needs is a reinforcement made of strong paper round the opening. The balloon can be transported folded up.

Now open it up over the fire. Here you must be very careful even though nothing much can happen if the balloon catches fire, but it is a pity to waste the work you have put in to it. For the first attempt the flame of a Bunsen burner or a camping stove is suitable. The launch can take place in a high room or on a stairway. Place a non-combustible base under the burner: a baking tray, for instance. Over the burner place a stove pipe with a slit in it (figure 126). The slit allows fresh air in to the burner.

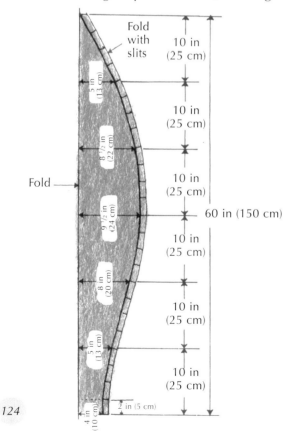

Fold with slits

10 in (25 cm)

5 in (13 cm)

10 in (25 cm)

8 1/2 in (22 cm)

Fold

10 in (25 cm)

9 1/2 in (24 cm)

60 in (150 cm)

10 in (25 cm)

8 in (20 cm)

10 in (25 cm)

5 in (13 cm)

10 in (25 cm)

4 in (10 cm)

2 in (5 cm)

124

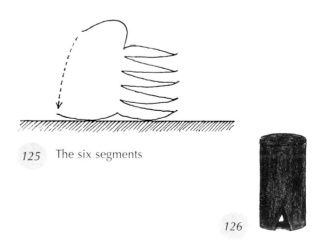

125   The six segments

126

For launching you need a crew of two. One holds the balloon at the top and one at the bottom. Open the balloon high above the flame, and the hot air will fill it out. Now lower the balloon slowly, watching carefully until the flame is inside the balloon. After a few moments it will rise by itself. In the excitement do not forget your naked flame.

Out of doors the launching is not so simple. You can only launch on days when there is no wind, or a faint current of air, so where possible choose a sheltered spot. It is also helps if lots of spectators make a close circle round the launching spot. Use a camping stove, or you can try an open wood fire. In the latter case, wait until the flames die down but the embers are still glowing. Rake the embers well together. A good idea is to take a piece of tin bent round to make a pipe with air vents at the bottom. A stove pipe is too narrow. At a garden party I saw a balloon launched successfully over a fire in a barrel.

Naturally one would not make a fire in the woods because of the danger of causing a forest fire, and anyway the ascending balloon (and your view of it) would be hampered by the trees. Open countryside is best for this purpose. See that there are no roads nearby as the balloon could distract drivers when it comes down again.

It is possible that the balloon will tilt to one side when it is rising, or even turn upside down letting out all the hot air. In this case the balloon will have to be weighted below, perhaps with a clothes peg, or with a basket hung by a fine thread in which a light doll rides.

The suggested measurements of the balloon can be increased or reduced on the same scale. Unless you take a lighter kind of tissue paper, the strips should not be shorter than 3 feet (1 m) otherwise the balloon will be too heavy in proportion to its volume. If you double the measurements the balloon is four times as heavy but it will take eight times as much hot air. The balloon then rises much better but it is also more flimsy.

Never launch the balloon with a fire attached below it because it is obviously too dangerous. By taking suitable precautions the trouble of making the balloon will certainly be rewarded by fine flights.

127

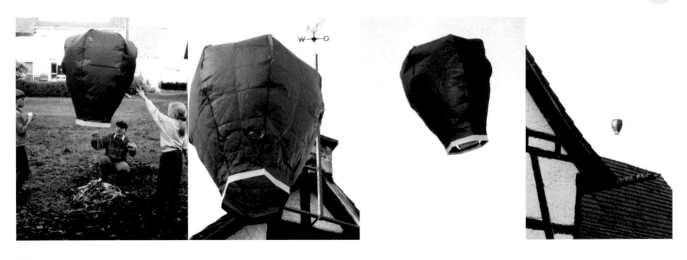

The sun balloon

You may be able to buy this toy ready-made. It is shaped like a thick black sausage made of especially light cellophane. Simply lay the air-filled sausage in the sun. The black colour quickly absorbs the sun's warmth conducting it to the air inside. This expands making the balloon buoyant and it rises. You should keep it anchored by a string so that it does not fly away. It should only be launched when there is no wind. With this balloon the heat is not taken from earthly fire but from the sun.

Bimetallic seesaw

Bimetallic strips are wonderful things. They are metal strips either wound up like a watch-spring or extended flat. In either case, as the name implies, the strip consists of two different metals joined firmly together. When they are heated the two metals expand at different rates with the result that the strip bends or the spiral unwinds or winds up tighter. When the metal cools the opposite movement takes place.

Here is how you can make a fine toy with a bimetallic spiral. Make a seesaw on to which you can later place two little men. Place a night light over the point of support of the seesaw. Set a wire bow on the seesaw stretched over the night light. Join one end of the bimetallic spiral to the wire bow. Solder a piece of wire on to the other end of the spiral. Fit a bead on to the other end of the wire. The bead acts as a weight. Now arrange the device in such a way that the spiral is positioned exactly over the wick when at rest and the bead lies to one side with its weight held by a stop (figure 128). The seesaw will be down on that side. Now light the night light. The flame will heat the spiral which brings the bead on to the other

128

side and the seesaw goes down on that side. In that position the spiral cools down as it is now lying beside the flame. The bead goes back to its first position and the seesaw rocks back again. Then the whole thing starts all over again.

It is a pleasant toy to watch, perhaps at teatime when it is growing dark, but my congratulations to the craftsman who succeeds in constructing this finely balanced contraption.

The sounding pipe

Take a piece of stove pipe about 3 feet long (1 m). Take some fine wire mesh and insert it into one end of the pipe up to about one third of its length. Heat the mesh with the powerful flame of a blow lamp or a camping gas stove, until the mesh is glowing hot. Now hold the pipe upright and remove it from the flame. In a few moments it will begin to sound, astonishingly long and persistently. The hot air rising in the pipe makes spirals above the mesh and causes the vibrations in the pipe which we hear. You might describe it as an organ pipe blown by fire.

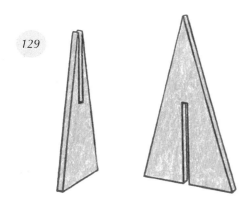
129

130

Shadow games

Everyone has sat in the dark and had a light in front of them. Near at hand was an object, behind the object it was quite dark, and there were shadows. If you moved the light carefully you could see how the shadows always moved away from the light. That is obvious of course, but if you observe this moving of the shadows you may well be tempted to make a game out of it. This is how, after much trial and error, the forest shadow game came about.

Take a piece of cardboard as the base. Colour it like the ground in the woods. On it paint paths consisting of circles as big as the base of the night light which you are going to use. Now make some trees, for example, by taking two pointed bits of plywood with slots so that they can be fitted together in the form of a cross (figure 129). Paint these trees in the right colours and place them on the base where there are no paths. Take a dice and some counters such as little playing figures from a board game.

When it gets dark in the room we can start. A grown-up directs the light. They light the night light and place it anywhere on the path. The trees now cast their shadows. The grown-up directing the game now closes their eyes and the children hide the counters (they are the dwarfs) in the shadows of the trees. After that the light director throws the dice and moves the light that number of circles in any direction. If a dwarf is lit up he is found. Which dwarf can stay hidden the longest?

The game can be developed further. The dwarfs are allowed to run away from the light but they must keep in the shadow. After every move the light director shuts his eyes and the dwarfs hide again, but they are not allowed to cross any strip of light however narrow on the floor of the wood.

If the game does not come to an end it is because there are too many trees and you must take some away.

One tree can be chosen as the den, and any dwarf getting into it by keeping in the shadow is safe. Now try making the condition that all the dwarfs have to meet under a particular tree without coming into the light. If a dwarf does get into the light he can be freed if another can get to him in the shadow. Until then he is under a spell and cannot move.

These are some variations to the 'forest shadow game', a play of light and shadow. Other shadow games can no doubt be invented.

To get coloured shadows you need two candles and a piece of transparent coloured cellophane. Near the two candles place an object, such as a matchbox. It will cast two shadows. Where they both overlap it is quite dark: this is called the 'umbra'. The lighter shadows are called 'penumbrae', the half-shadows, because each is lit up by only one of the lights. The shadows are seen best on white paper laid on the table as a base.

Now hold a piece of coloured cellophane, say a red one, in front of the brighter flame. The surroundings are immediately coloured red including the penumbra of the other candle. The penumbra of the red candle is a faint green even though there is no green light! If one of the candle lights is coloured green the shadow will be red. Red and green are complementary colours. In a similar way blue and orange, yellow and purple complement each other.

What happens when both candles have a coloured strip held in front of them? Then you have coloured shadows. It is worthwhile playing with them in the way described. You can even colour the light of three candles and study the many shades of colour. It would be fun to develop this, perhaps making a coloured shadow theatre.

131

The rainbow

To conclude this section I would like to mention another remarkable phenomenon. Dewdrops sometimes sparkle in colour in the sunshine, also the rainbow gets its colours from drops, from the falling rain, but there is another way of seeing the seven colours of the rainbow. The flame of a candle appears in the colours red, orange, yellow, green, turquoise, blue and violet when you look at it through a glass prism. To do this you will have to stand a few yards away from the candle and look quite a bit to one side, turning the prism until you find the coloured flame. In the beginning you will need some patience.

The prism can be made of perspex (plexiglass), which is cheap. Real glass prisms are expensive but give better colours. Look carefully at other things in the surroundings: everywhere where light and darkness meet colours arise. If you watch attentively you will find a new colour which cannot be seen in the candle, a glorious bright purple.

When the room is properly darkened you can do it differently. Place the prism about 3 feet (1 m) away from the candle, and at some distance further behind the prism and place a white sheet of paper to one side. If everything has been arranged skilfully a delicate part of the rainbow will appear on the paper. The paper should be in the shadow.

This will also be possible in sunlight. Place the prism on the window ledge and you will see the colours on the floor. It is more beautiful if the prism is held horizontally on an edge. You can make a suitable stand for it (figure 132). The piece of rainbow appears on the opposite wall and moves with the sun.

132   Horizontal prism on an edge

The spectrum from a prism   133

The sun's rays

The sun's rays are invisible, but you can still play with them. You just need a mirror. And we're not talking about annoying a teacher with dancing light spots or dazzling someone!

A mirror will reflect the sun's rays around a corner, and several mirrors around several corners. So you can let the sun's light shine into some dark spots like a basement or cellar. It's no use fixing the mirror, as the sun moves surprisingly quickly, so someone has to hold the mirror and direct the light on to the next mirror.

At the end you can set up a prism as described above and see a rainbow in the dark.

Lightning trees

134

Never play with lightning! Flying a kite in thundery weather can be fatal. But it is worth watching lightning from afar, and at night it can be especially dramatic.

Keep your eyes open when walking through woods and you will often see the trace on a tree where lightning has struck. Recent strikes are obvious (figure 134). Solitary trees are more likely to be struck.

Extinguishing a fire

What's the best way to put a fire out? Every child will immediately answer, 'with water.' And that's true, of course, provided there's enough water around. It's quite a sight to watch the fire hissing and steaming.

Air can also extinguish a fire — after all, we blow out a candle or a match. But then we also blow to make flames come out of a glow, because we know that fire needs air. So only small flames or fires can be blown out. Large fires are made worse by the wind, and they start producing their own wind as can be seen with forest fires.

You can also use earth to put a fire out. Earth cools and stops air from getting to the fire. Try putting the picnic fire out with sand or earth.

4. Playing with Air

Just as water invites us to bathe and to immerse ourselves in it, so air invites us primarily to breathe it, testing it for its fragrance and moisture. But breathing out can be real play, for instance: blowing boats and balls over obstacles or along a channel made ourselves with two wires as in mini golf (figure 135), or there is an amusing game where everyone sits round a table and on the word 'go' starts to blow some light object like a piece of cotton wool. When the cotton wool finally sticks to someone that person has to pay a forfeit. Rather than playing against each other I would recommend trying to achieve a common goal such as keeping a ball for as long as possible on a sloping table by blowing.

Although essentially a light element, air can develop quite a power, as in wind and storm. Sometimes the air is so strong that we can lean against it. It is good to take children to see the power of the wind and the waves by the sea, an experience long to be remembered. When the air is calm we can create wind by running. Many games need still air, and we can begin with these games.

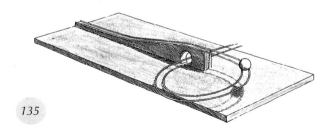

135

Blowing soap bubbles

These delicate objects are a wonder. As well as the marvel that they can float in the air they glisten in special colours, particularly red and green, but not in all the colours of the rainbow. The following has proved a good recipe for making the soap solution: cut kitchen soap into shavings and dissolve them in warm water. If possible add some drops of glycerine. Use a drinking straw. Dip it in and blow. With care and practice you will soon be able to send up beautiful big soap bubbles into the air. The trick is to stop blowing just before the bubble bursts. The bubble is in danger of bursting when colourless patches begin to form. Soap bubbles will show the least air movement. They will rise above a radiator or over a burning candle.

136

The air balloon

The air balloon is filled with a light gas and held by a string. Indoors you can hang light objects on it such as baskets made of paper in which you can put very light dolls (such as those made of cotton wool or wool) so that they get carried up to the ceiling. An air balloon of the usual size will not stand carrying much ballast. With some skill and a lot of patience you can get the balloon to float without rising or sinking like the submarine and fish described on page 57. The air in the room must be quite still.

If you let go of the balloon in the open air you will certainly not see it again, for it will go on rising higher and higher, growing smaller and smaller until you can see it no longer. Somewhere and at some time or other it will come down again. Sometimes a competition is run with air balloons to see whose can be carried the farthest. A label is attached with the sender's address and a request to the finder to inform them of the place where it was found. Sometimes the balloons travel a remarkably long way. (see also The hot-air balloon on p. 77).

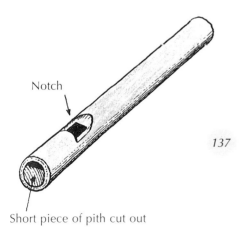

Notch

137

Short piece of pith cut out

Sounds from air

By blowing you can also make musical sounds. You only need a key with a hole in it. If you blow sharply across the edge it will give out a shrill whistle; very often you can get more than one note. You can develop this simple principle by arranging a series of pipes of different lengths made of metal or thin bamboo. The pipes must be closed at the bottom. To make a true scale in this way is not easy. In the case of bamboo pipes we have something like a simple Pan flute. But it is quicker and simpler to take a series of bottles of the same size and fill them to various levels with water. You cannot really play a tune on these, because the bottles are too clumsy and the necks are not close enough together.

This is the way to make a proper pipe: take a fresh willow twig a good 4 inches long (10 cm). Cut a little notch in the bark (see figure 137). Now tap the bark all round with the back of a knife and the pith can be withdrawn from the bark. We have to get the air stream to strike against the hole made by the notch. Now remove the pith from the notch to the mouthpiece, cut the pith flat on top and insert it again into the bark-pipe so that the air stream strikes exactly against the cut, and the little whistle is ready. You can stick the rest of the pith in the bottom end, and by moving it in and out you can tune the pipe to a given note.

Humming wood

It is well worth reviving this ancient toy. Simply take a piece of wood, a good hand-span long and two fingers broad, for instance, from the side of an old ladder. Bore a hole in one end and tie a piece of string as long as your arm through the hole. The hole must not be in the middle, but that usually happens anyway. Now swing the wood on the end of the string round and round either horizontally over your head or vertically — it does not matter which — it will begin to sound. Some skill is necessary to make it hum. After a time it will stop humming because the wood has twisted the string, and you must let it unwind before you can get the wood to hum again. If you bore holes in the wood (figure 139) you will increase the sound. Whirling is a game for outside.

Quite an ordinary piece of wood can be used for whirling and then cast loose. Shape it like a ruler 8 to 12 inches long (20 to 30 cm), 1 1/2 to 2 inches wide (3 to 5 cm), fairly thin (about 1/5 in, 5 mm).

The wood must be thrown skilfully. When it is released it must be given a spin (figure 140). You will need practice. Once you have mastered the art of throwing, the wood will rise into the air and give off a humming noise. Heavy wood will hum for longer than light wood, but light wood will fly longer. Long strips of paper will also fly, rotating fast, and flutter down silently to the ground. That is fun too.

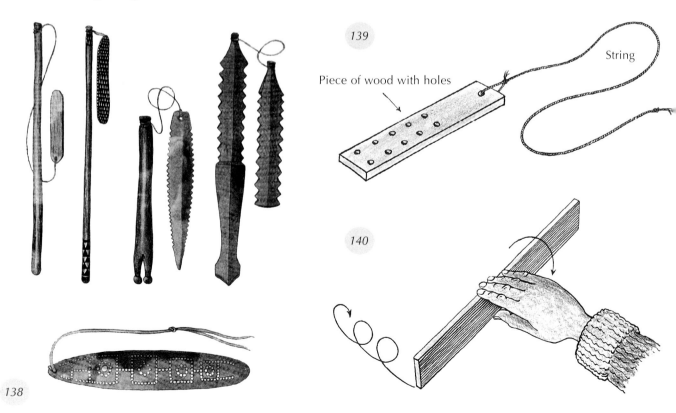

139

Piece of wood with holes

String

140

138

86

The humming button

An indoor game is the humming button. Take as big a button as possible, thread some good button thread about 2 feet long (60 cm) through the holes and tie the ends together so that you now have a loop (figure 141). Hold the loop between your hands wound round two fingers on each hand with the button well into the middle. Start the button spinning by drawing the thread tightly and rhythmically after giving the button a few turns to start it off. The thread will twist itself more and more each time and the button will rotate faster and faster, first one way then the other, and it will hum softly but quite clearly. If more holes are bored near the edge of the button it will sing even louder.

Mobiles

You can easily make a mobile yourself. Mobiles are pendants which move in the slightest current of air. The motifs can be birds, butterflies, bees, sailing boats, fish, and so on. Make the objects first and take care that they are not too heavy. Lightweight coloured paper is suitable. Then suspend the motifs by fine thread from little rods or thin wire. If the latter are slightly curved the task is easier. To assemble them begin at the bottom. Take a short rod and hang the first two objects at each end. Tie a thread at the point of balance, and tie the other end of the thread to the end of a somewhat longer rod. Balance this rod with another object at the other end. Continue in this fashion until the mobile is big enough. Take care that the objects suspended cannot touch each other as the rods turn (figure 142).

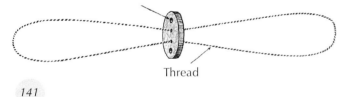

Additional holes in button

Thread

141

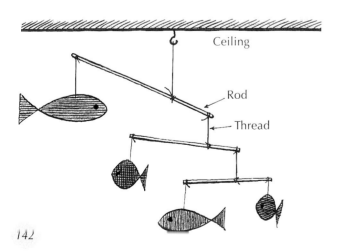

Ceiling

Rod

Thread

142

143

Paper darts

There are all kinds of paper darts. Even a postcard can fly if it is folded over lengthwise once or twice and weighted with a paper clip (figure 144). You have to experiment with patience and learn to launch it, and eventually it will work. If the card plummets down steeply it is too heavy in front: push the clip in or unfold one of the folds. If it will not fly straight pull the clip out a bit. By moving the clip you alter the point of balance: an airman's old adage says, 'You can fly with a barn door if you get the point of balance right.' This rule applies to all paper darts.

To remind you of the art of making paper darts, which perhaps you learned at school, figures 145 a to h show the sequence of folds for a good model.

If you fly the darts out of the window they sometimes get into an up-current and fly into the window above us. You can only hope your neighbour enjoys the fun!

Finally, you may want to build bigger flying models, proper ones with a wooden frame, but you have to be capable of fine workmanship.

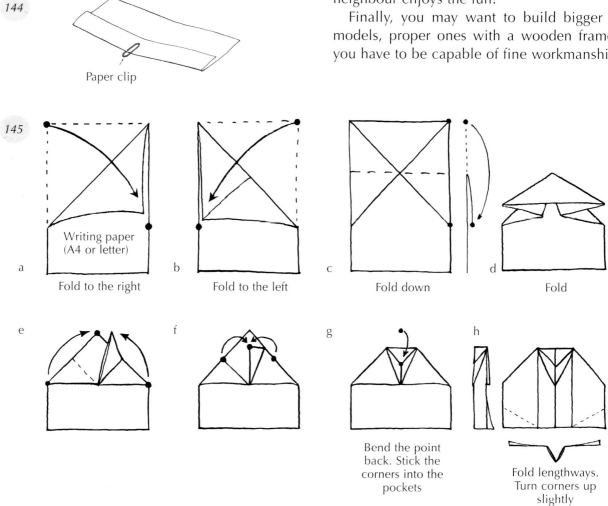

144

Paper clip

145

a Fold to the right

Writing paper (A4 or letter)

b Fold to the left

c Fold down

d Fold

e

f

g Bend the point back. Stick the corners into the pockets

h Fold lengthways. Turn corners up slightly

The wind ball

You can build a ball which can be borne lightly by the wind and is also suitable as a pendant on a mobile. Cut the three parts out of light cardboard (it is good if this is coloured) according to figure 146 (diameter about 4 inches, 10 cm). Fold along the dotted lines, stick together, and the wind ball is finished.

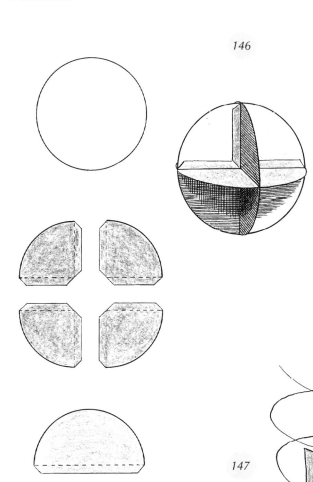

146

Parachutes

Before you go into a shop and start buying, look around in nature. There are various seeds that can fly. The best example is the dandelion head. When you blow it lots of little parachutes float away. Then there are seeds of trees which you don't need to blow, but just throw them into the air or let them fall: sycamore, maple, fir, spruce and lime. These seeds have wings which cause them to rotate like helicopter rota blades.

In the Malay Archipelago there is a plant, the zanonia, whose seeds are real gliders flying long distances like the postcard we have described.

A strip of paper, split at one end, with the flaps folded outwards and slightly twisted will fall gently to the ground turning slowly (figure 147), just like the seeds mentioned. It is fun to let these spin down whole flights of stairs. You can make a proper little parachute out of a square piece of lightweight cloth about the size of a pocket handkerchief. Tie a fine thread to each corner, and knot the loose ends of the threads together. Attach a little weight, for instance, a nail, which can be the parachutist, or you can use a little doll. But the size of the cloth and the weight must be in relation to each other (figure 148).

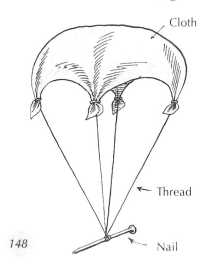

Cloth

Thread

Nail

147

148

Helicopters

In Japan there is a simple toy made of bamboo called Také-tombo. Sometimes you can find something similar in the West, though none is as simple and effective as the Japanese version. However, it can be made easily at home.

Take a thin board about 4 inches long (10 cm) and cut it out in the shape of a propeller. It does not have to be bamboo, although this kind of wood is particularly durable. Bore a hole in the centre of the propeller and glue the end of a thin round rod into the hole. The rod should be about the same length as the propeller (figure 149). Now take the rod of the propeller between the palms of your hands and spin it. If you do this quickly and skilfully, when you let go, the propeller will fly up to quite a height before it starts to fall again. This is a simple game for outside, because the spinning propeller can cause damage inside a room.

Another kind of helicopter is quite harmless and can be launched safely inside a room, but it is more difficult to construct. Take a rod about 8 inches (20 cm) long and fix a bent bit of tin at one end as a mounting. A glass bead acts as the axle of the propeller. The axle is driven by an engine made of two elastic bands. These elastic bands are secured to the other end of the rod, where a second propeller is fixed. This propeller must be pitched in the opposite direction (figure 150). The elastic engine is wound up by turning the movable propeller with a finger. When you let the whole thing go it will fly up to the ceiling where it will try, like an insect, to crawl along until the elastic bands have unwound and it falls down again. For the contraption to work as we have described, all parts should be made as light as possible. The rod can be made of balsa wood, the mounting from very thin tin, 1/100 in (0.2 mm) wire for the axle, bristles with tissue paper stretched between them for the propellers. Alternatively, the second propeller could be mounted directly under the first; it turns with the rod in the opposite direction to the first.

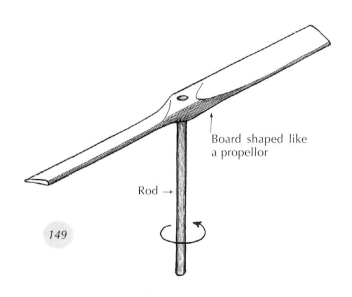

Board shaped like a propellor

Rod →

149

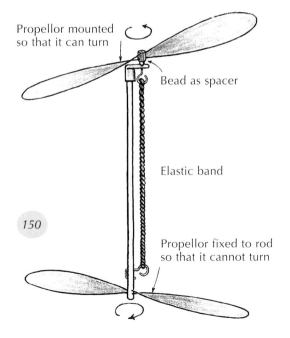

Propellor mounted so that it can turn

Bead as spacer

Elastic band

150

Propellor fixed to rod so that it cannot turn

Wind wheels and propellers

The 'helicopters' described above actually do have propellers, with a vertical axle, but it is easier to play with propellers with horizontal axles. The simplest is the wind wheel, which you can buy at the fair. But you can also make it yourself; big, little, coloured or white, just as you like. You need a square tough piece of paper. Cut in at the four corners diagonally and fold over the four flaps (figure 151). With a pin pierce each of the four flaps as well as the centre. Insert the pin through a bead to act as a spacer and push the pin into a stick. Then the wind wheel is ready. It will turn in the wind itself. When there is no wind a child can run with it, holding it up in the air and it will turn too. This is the simplest form of construction. If the toy is to last longer you need a stronger construction.

152

Cut diagonals into square paper, turn flaps inwards, insert pin through middle.

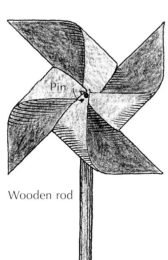

Pin

Wooden rod

151

It was the custom when I was a child to have a propeller on your bicycle. The propeller was carved out of a thin piece of wood, with a knife. This will require a little skill. It is harder to fit the axle on to the bicycle and to get the bead to lie so that the propeller turns easily. Don't forget to oil the bearing. Remember also that propellers with little pitch turn faster when you are riding your bike. Of course the propeller does not drive, it is driven.

A proper windmill can be built without much trouble. The Dutch ones which you sometimes see in people's front gardens between garden gnomes are very realistic miniatures. However, the necessary amount of work and cost can easily be underestimated. The windmill illustrated here is a simpler model.

Sail windmills are recommended as patterns. The mounting can be an old cardboard drum or container. Make it look attractive by painting it or sticking coloured paper over it. Half fill with stones to make it stand firmly and prevent the wind blowing it over. Bore two holes opposite each other to take the axle which is a wooden rod about $1/2$ in (10 mm) thick (figure 153). On the windward side it needs a spacer (a round bead, for instance) like the wind wheel, and on the lee side you can fix a rimmed wheel like the waterwheel to drive a model. But first you must make the sails. You need a hub with some holes (you can get them in a model shop). This is glued on to the axle. Insert rods of equal length into the holes. Cut out the triangular sails from a piece of cloth, sew a thread to each corner and tie them at the three corners to the rods (figure 154). If the bearing lets the axle runs easily the mill will work in a light current of air, and with a fresh wind it will go whizzing round. The workmanship does not need to be exact, but the bearing should be good; you can use metal or synthetic tubes stuck into the cardboard. To roof the mill you can give it a conical hat.

153

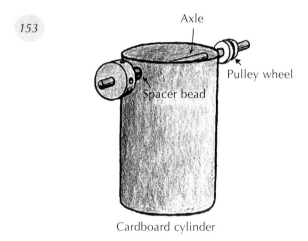

Axle

Pulley wheel

Spacer bead

Cardboard cylinder

155

154

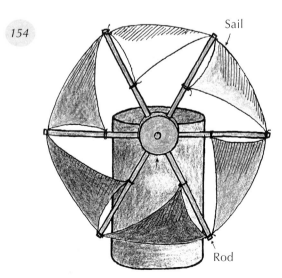

Sail

Rod

Horizontal wind wheels

Horizontal wind wheels have the advantage that they can turn in whatever direction the wind comes from.

Fix some paper funnels onto a bicycle wheel and we have a simple horizontal wind wheel (figure 157). An even simpler construction just uses some bent tin. A flat piece will never turn in the wind, but bent into an S-shape the wind will find more resistance on the hollow side than on the convex surface. The axle can be vertical or horizontal (in which case it must be at right angles to the wind direction). Bend a suitable bit of tin, not too small, into shape. Either solder or superglue a metal tube onto the middle and mount on a pencil. If the metal is shiny it will work as a scarecrow (figure 156).

The same principle is used in the two half tines of the Savonius rotor (figure 158).

157

158

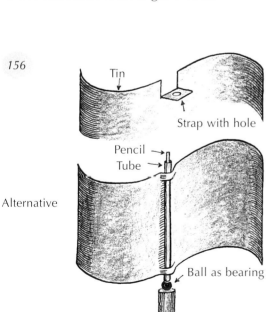

156

Tin

Strap with hole

Pencil

Tube

Alternative

Ball as bearing

A simple rotor consists of a horizontal stick mounted on a vertical axle. Stick a foil to each end of the horizontal stick (figures 159 & 160). The wind will bend the foils sufficiently to start turning the rotor.

A light wind is enough to drive a prayer wheel. With a jigsaw cut two plywood discs and cut some angled slits around the edge. To ensure the slits of the two discs line up you can use a simple geometric construction. Draw a circle with a pair of compasses, and using the same radius mark off the six points on the circumference. Then connect as shown. From each point, saw halfway along the line (figure 162).

Cut a large hole in the centre of the lower disc and set a bearing into the centre of the upper disk. The bearing can be a tiny plastic, metal or even glass cup.

Now cut six strips as wide as the slits are deep. The strips can be stiff paper or card, but to make the prayer wheel last in all weathers plastic, nylon or even tin is better. Pull the strips through the slits and stick them to the discs. Use a knitting needle or thick wire stuck in the ground as the axle. The prayer wheel will turn because of the angled foils (figure 161).

159

160

161

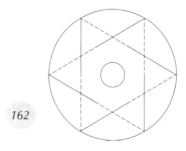

162

Weathervanes

The weathervane (weathercock) often has the shape of a plane with a propeller. You can make one and put the aircraft on a pole in the garden. To ensure that the plane will point properly into the wind the tail must be relatively large. Behind the propeller and underneath the aircraft put a bead as a spacer to decrease the friction of the axle. The plane should be mounted at its point of balance (figure 163). Build the plane itself as best you can from wood, paint it in bright colours or use a transparent varnish to protect it. This is important for the weathervane should last for some considerable time in wind and weather. You could also make a weathercock, but without a propeller of course.

Another instrument for scaring away unwanted feathered guests is the Klapotez. The wine growers of Styria in Austria use this type of weathervane which makes a noise when it turns. Clappers on a crankshaft hammer on to a sounding board. The wind drives eight thin laths, each about 3 feet (1 m) long, fixed into the axle and set at an angle. The contraption is held into the wind by a broom sticking out behind, and is quite a big unit (figure 165).

A bicycle wheel will make a good windmill if the spokes are covered cleverly (figure 166). Look at the picture carefully to see how it is done. The angle of the 'blades' becomes steeper towards the centre which works efficiently.

Optically, any of the windmills show an unusual effect if two wheels mounted behind each other turn in opposite directions. When the wind blows the blades shimmer, especially if they are coloured.

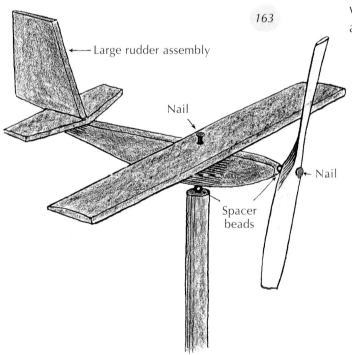

163

Large rudder assembly

Nail

Nail

Spacer beads

164

165

166

167

The running wheel

The last things which we have described were of a passive kind, that is to say the activity was all in the construction. Once the gadget is finished after much toil and trouble it runs by itself, and you can only watch it. It is quite different with the running wheel, because you have to run hard with it, as it is blown along by the wind. But you will need not only wind but lots of space, best of all a long stretch of sandy beach. If you go to such a place with your children take a piece of cardboard cut into a circle, the bigger the better. Cut triangles into it and bend out the triangles on alternate sides (figure 168). The wind will catch these protruding triangles and blow the wheel along, possibly for miles.

An Oloid (figure 169) is simple to make. Just cut a slit into each of two discs. Stick them together so that the inner rim reaches the centre of the other. They will wobble along strangely in the wind.

Wind-driven bogeys

Sail bogeys are often seen on beaches. You can make model ones. It is important that the wheels, usually three, should be set wide apart, so that the bogey is broad in the beam. You can take either wood or metal for the job. You can also buy kits to assemble. The wheels are bought ready-made, and you can get some with solid rubber tyres. The model does not need to have a wheel that can be steered. Set the mast slightly forward of the middle of the bodywork and rig it. It is not difficult to rig a sail, but it must be able to swivel so as to lie to the wind properly. It can be set by adjustable strings (figure 170). The biggest problem can be finding a good windy place for the bogey. A sandy beach is often slightly uneven which does not affect a big craft, but can slow down a small model. A street is suitable if there are no cars on it. So it is not advisable to start building a sailing bogey unless you know where you can try it out.

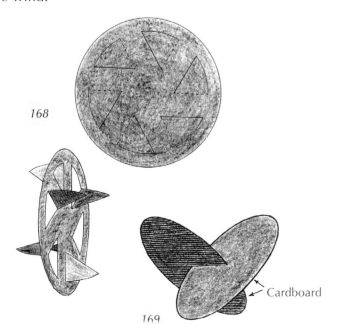

168

169 Cardboard

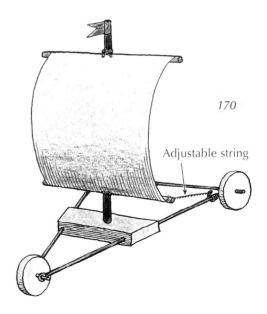

170

Adjustable string

A frozen lake or pond is very good. If you mount it on runners instead of wheels you have a sailing sledge. In this case the sledge will only sail before the wind, as the runners do not prevent side-slip like wheels or a keel on a boat.

A propeller bogey is also fun. It is constructed on the same lines as the helicopter described on page 90, but instead of the second propeller you construct a wire undercarriage (figures 171 & 172). This contraption will shoot along for quite a distance provided it can run on a smooth flat surface.

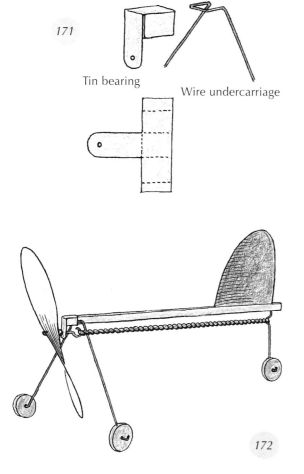

171

Tin bearing

Wire undercarriage

172

Kites

And so we come to the kite. The greatest fun is making it, so resist buying it ready-made. You can make the kite square, rectangular, hexagonal, like a trapeze, round, single-storeyed or double-storeyed ... as you choose. You can make it coloured, you can paint it or just have it plain. The frame is built of strong but light rods. Pine rods or bamboo sticks are suitable. You can take thin bamboo sticks, or you can split thicker ones and use the leftovers in the construction. I shall describe briefly the construction of a kite on classical lines. Tie two rods of almost the same length together in the form of a cross, the shorter rod placed in the front, a third of the way down the longer rod. A taut string tied and glued to the notched ends of the four rods holds the cross in position. Greaseproof paper is then stretched over this frame. This paper is quite light but does not tear too easily. Cloth is stronger but it lets the wind through. It will only work in areas where you can count on strong winds.

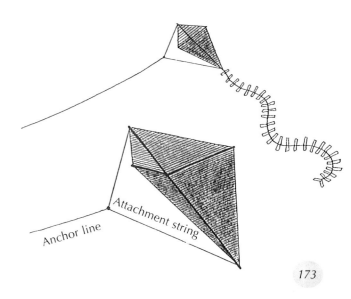

Attachment string

Anchor line

173

Every kite builder should know that the kite must not be hollow or concave below. By nature this will happen as the fabric tends to belly in the wind. This shape will rise well, but it crashes back down to earth, and you won't get much joy out of it. This defect can be avoided by giving the kite a slight V-form (figure 173). With this shape it will not rise so well, but once it is up it will hold its position stably in the wind. To prevent the fabric from bellying, fix it to the bottom of the frame. To obtain the V-form, bend the cross-piece or fix a string to the ends of the cross-piece and draw it tight. Tie a string to the head and tail end. Then tie the line to this string towards the head third. With stronger winds it can be tied nearer the middle, in gentler winds more towards the front.

It is dangerous to fly a kite near power lines or near an airfield.

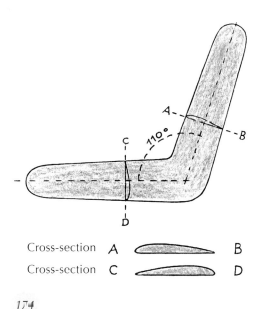

Cross-section   A   B
Cross-section   C   D

174

The boomerang

The boomerang is properly a piece of sporting equipment. It was used by the aborigines of Australia as a hunting weapon. You may be able to find it in sports shops. To learn the art of throwing the boomerang yourself you will need a lot of space. Send away spectators in case you injure them, because initially the boomerang will certainly not come back to the thrower. Once you have some practice, and can gauge the wind your boomerang will fly in a surprisingly wide circle — turning all the time — and come back in a spiral to its starting point. Some people can catch a boomerang in flight without getting all bruised.

The boomerang phenomenon is physically possible because of the shape of the wood in cross-section which is like the wing of a plane: curved above and flat below (figure 174). The rotation causes it to maintain its height. You can try to shape the wood yourself. Good plywood is suitable. Begin with small models in order to gather experience for bigger ones.

Sailing boats

The possibilities here are endless. The sailing boat combines playing with water and playing with air. There are sailing boats for all kinds of occasions, ages, technical ability, craftsmanship and materials. I shall select a few examples.

You can make a sailing boat from a walnut shell which is suitable for a bowl or the bath. You can take a match for a mast and fix it with wax or modelling material, some paper for a sail and glue it to the mast (figure 175) and now you can blow the ship along. Tiny dolls can ride in the boat. If you have a bigger bath or a basin you can build a harbour at each end, an island of moss and stones with a lighthouse on it and already shipping can be in full swing. Many parents will allow a little birthday candle to burn in the nutshell. In this case you can't have a sail and you have to blow with very great care.

Playing outside in the open air by a pool is even better. Already the simplest boat will sail with the wind. You can make the hulls from bits of pine bark, with a little stick as a mast set slightly forward of the ship's middle. You can make the step (the hole to take the mast) with a penknife. A dry leaf is the sail stuck into the mast. If necessary a thin thread can hold mast and sail in position.

← Matchstick

← Paper sail

175

176

Do not glue, but tie, that's more natural. You can even use a grass stalk instead of the thread. With a penknife in your pocket and technical imagination in your head you can build boats by the pond with whatever natural materials can be found there. If the wind blows your ship away it doesn't matter for you will soon build another.

If you have time at home to prepare for playing by the water the boat can look something like this. Cut a board with a pointed end. Bore a hole in it forward of the middle. Put a stick in for a mast. Take a square piece of cloth to make a square-rigged Viking sail, or a triangular piece to make a lateen sail or even two sails. At the stern fix a simple rudder which can be turned or bent. You might fit a keel and the boat is ready. The wind will drive the vessel over the water. Again dolls can travel on it if the doll's mother will allow it. But accidents can happen! The wind can blow the boat over to an inaccessible part of the pond. To avoid this you can tie a long line on to the boat and pull it back by the line. I once saw a little boat without a line get caught in some weeds and two clever children stretched a line right across the pond and carefully retrieved their boat.

A sailing boat can easily capsize. The outrigger boats of the South Sea islanders do not capsize, nor do modern catamarans (figure 176). Once I saw two brothers, each making a hull. The hulls were then fixed together, with a fine sail, and in this way a boat was built in harmonious partnership. For the catamaran's hulls you can take two plastic bottles which, though not very beautiful, is very much quicker. Of course, they must be empty and properly sealed. They are joined by three boards, one forward, one aft and one midships with the mast firmly fixed to it, and well rigged. Now the craft is ready for launching.

But if you are not going to sail with the wind you will need a keel to prevent the boat from being blown sideways.

With skill you can build a model yacht with a keel and good rigging. With a radio-controlled rudder and boom you can sail against the wind (figure 177).

177

Cable cars

This subject is treated more fully in the first part 'Playing with The Earth', so I shall only mention it here since cable cars run high up in the air. For the supporting cable stretch a piece of string from the leg of the table to the window catch; from a post in the garden to the balcony; from a big stone to a tree; or from one window to another; over a ditch or hollow. The car is soon built: depending on the size required, for the bottom you can take a matchbox, a cigar box, a shoebox, or even a light wooden vegetable box. At each end of this open container tie a loop of string with a ring in the middle. Pass the cable through the two rings. A second string is fastened to the two rings. This is the hauling cable (figure 178). Now the car is ready to convey dolls and small freight. To do this, pull the hauling cable. Admittedly a traveller with pulley wheels would be better and more realistic, but much more difficult to make. The rings do have one advantage: the ring traveller rides absolutely surely, it can never come off

178

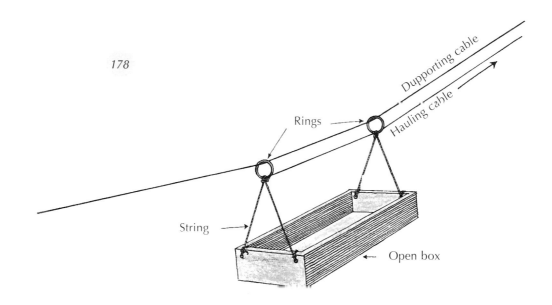

Dupporting cable

Hauling cable

Rings

String

Open box

the cable and fall to the ground. If there is not enough slope on the cable and the car gets stuck you can tie a second hauling cable to pull the car downhill. This can be joined to the first cable to make a continuous hauling cable. You can only have intermediate supports if the car has a traveller with pulley wheels. That kind of car just rolls down into the valley by itself, but it must be stopped gently.

Finally you can let a traveller run on its own. If a car is attached it must have two pulley wheels. If the traveller runs by itself one wheel is sufficient, but it will need a weight to stabilize it, as for instance two wooden slats (figure 181). You can easily make a traveller from one of the usual modelling kits. Now sling up a long cord. It should hang a bit slack then the wheel will run on and up the other end and back down once more. A craftsman can also make a figure such as a cyclist to ride on the cord.

179

180

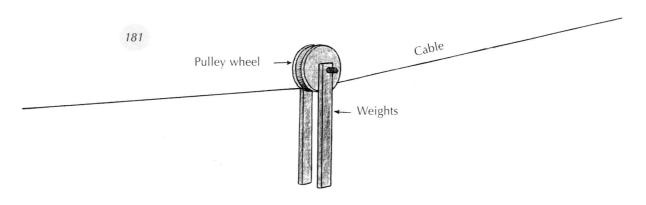

181

Pulley wheel →

Cable

← Weights

And finally a game of skill

Take a piece of bamboo and cut it so that one end is open and the other closed by a knot. Near the knot drill a small hole and glue a small (metal) tube into it. If you blow into the bamboo rod air will come out of the little tube. Now take a ball of cotton wool and put a wire through the middle. One end of the wire is fashioned into a little hook, the other is inserted into the tube. If you blow now the cotton wool ball will rise and when the wire rises out of the tube it will fall away.

Attach a wire ring at a suitable height (figure 182). Now the challenge is to hook the ball onto the wire ring without using your hands, just by blowing. With some practice you should manage.

183

182

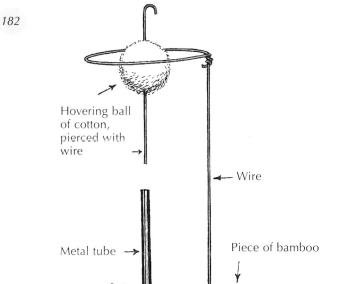

Hovering ball of cotton, pierced with wire →

← Wire

Metal tube →

Piece of bamboo ↓

Closed →

← Blow

Conclusion

In this little book simple and more complicated models for home-construction have been described. They are all designed to bring us in contact with the living elements. I am not concerned with making exact replicas of life-size devices, but simply with making models that work. A replica model ship belongs in a glass case, it is not a toy, but an object for a museum. The elements themselves are a part of nature and they are all-important. On the other hand, we must not underrate our children's powers of imagination. A nutshell really is a little boat for them or a matchbox a cable car. To make the toys we do not generally need more than simple cheap materials. In the activity of construction you will gather all sorts of experience, for not every toy will work first time, and you will have to think and try out more ideas. Sometimes some expert advice and help will be necessary. But once you have made a mechanism and it functions as it should, that will double your joy, for then you are an expert and have mastered the problems involved.

This little book gives ideas for playing with the four ancient elements, earth, water, fire and air. The impetus to write down these ideas came from observing the joy of children when they encounter the elements and begin to play happily of their own accord.

I was also motivated to write this book because of anxiety concerning the future. While acknowledging the achievements of technology I maintain that what we have not yet learnt is to know how best to use our inventions. The computer is undoubtedly in the wrong place in the playroom, even though one can apparently play with it. It removes our children from reality to the extent that they can no longer do anything with the elements with which Nature surrounds us. This book is not against technology, on the contrary, it demonstrates a whole lot of simple, readily comprehensible technical practices. It shows the fundamental principles and it intends to help to prevent our consciousness of the four elements from becoming lost.

Another purpose underlies this book. We do not do our children any good by giving them ready-made toys. The child can, wants and ought to make efforts to succeed in situations which they can master. The whole range of ready-made (and expensive) toy machinery causes me considerable concern. Children who have been spoilt with these things may later manifest a demanding way of thinking: they will make demands on the outside world, but not on themselves. It is crucial for later life which toys our children experience.

May this book be a contribution to happy and serious play with the four elements.